BEHIND THE LINES

BEHIND THE LINES

★

A VETERAN QUARTERBACK'S
LOOK INSIDE THE NFL

Don Strock and Harvey Frommer

Introduction by Dan Marino

PHAROS BOOKS
A SCRIPPS HOWARD COMPANY
NEW YORK

First published in 1991.

Library of Congress Cataloging-in-Publication Data
Strock, Don.
 Behind the lines : a veteran quarterback's look
inside the NFL / Don Strock and Harvey Frommer.
  p.   cm.
 Includes index.
 ISBN 0-88687-539-0 : $17.95
 1. National Football League. 2. Sports—Social
aspects—United States. 3. Strock, Don. 4. Football players—United States—Biography. I. Frommer, Harvey. II. Title.
 GV955.5.N35S76 1991
 796.332'64'0973--dc20   91-12476   CIP

Pharos Books are available at special discounts on
bulk purchases for sales promotions, premiums,
fundraising or educational use. For details,
contact the Special Sales Department, Pharos
Books, 200 Park Avenue, New York, NY 10166.

Printed in the United States of America

Cover design: Todd Radom
Interior design: Janet Tingey

Pharos Books
A Scripps Howard Company
200 Park Avenue
New York, NY 10166

10 9 8 7 6 5 4 3 2 1

To my wife Debby,
who has always been there for me.

CONTENTS

ACKNOWLEDGMENTS

Various people and organizations gave time, direction, encouragement, and support to this project. I would like to especially thank the following:

my mother, Mabel Irene Strock, my father, David James Strock, Sr., my sister, Debra Jo, and my brother, David—for putting up with me through all the years;

Ralph Stringer; Jerry Kapstein, Henry Bernat, Jerry Claiborne, Charlie Coffey, Dan Henning, Henry Dunow, Myrna Frommer; Freddy Frommer; my in-laws, John and Helen Murrian;

the nice folks at Pharos—Howard Siner; and David Hendin; and Phil James for his fine copy editing;

the Marinos—Dan, Claire, Dano, Michael, and Joey;

many of my fellow teammates, the Calusa Country Club, Miami Herald, United Features;

Hollywood, our cat and our buddy;

a special thanks goes to Hana Lane, our editor at Pharos, whom I taught a lot about football and a person who taught me a lot about the world of publishing;

my biggest thank you goes to Harvey Frommer, who became not only my partner in this project but a good friend.

INTRODUCTION

by Dan Marino

I first met **Don Strock** back in 1983 when I was just a rookie joining the Miami Dolphins. He was a veteran quarterback, and I was just starting out. But we had instant rapport. Maybe it was the fact that we were both from Pennyslvania that helped a lot.

My rookie season and in the years after that I learned a great deal about the game of professional football and how to handle the position of quarterback from "Stroker." Only his friends call him that. In fact, Don probably taught me more about the art and science of being a National Football League quarterback than any other person I ever met.

Behind the Lines is a book that only "Stroker" could have written. His sense of humor, his honesty, his distinctive voice, his special feel for the people and places and politics of the game of football is interwoven throughout this book.

Some former athletes write books and they turn out to be interesting reading. *Behind the Lines* is riveting reading. There's so much inside stuff here—coaches, players, fans. There's so much about what goes on in the locker room, in the huddle, in the training camp.

There's information here that never appeared in print before. As the cliche goes, he tells it like it was and as it is.

My only complaint about the book is that Don ranked me behind Joe Willie Namath in his "Best of the Best" quarterbacks. I told you Stroker was honest—even to a fault.

If you want a book that will make you laugh, get you a little angry, tell you things about football that you never knew, *Behind the Lines* is for you. As Larry King said, "You won't be able to put *Behind the Lines* down." I know I couldn't. I'm looking forward to *Behind the Lines: Book II*.

KICKOFF

IF you're a football fan, I've got a lot to talk to you about. I've written this book for all of you who follow the NFL and wonder what it's really like on the inside. It's a game for money and for pride. It's also one that has its moments of great drama, high performance, enormous courage under pressure, zany doings, and wacky characters. We'll get into all of that.

Contrary to rumors, I never backed up Sammy Baugh, but you probably remember me as the guy who stood on the sidelines next to Don Shula so much of the time through fifteen years with the Miami Dolphins. I was the guy holding the clipboard, wearing the mesh baseball cap, sporting that deep Florida tan who gave all those funny hand signals. I even played—did I ever play! I also put in some time with the Cleveland Browns and the Indianapolis Colts. Seventeen years in all—a long time, long enough to put me in the top ten for longevity of all the quarterbacks who ever played the game. And hardly anyone else played for a longer time in a Miami Dolphins uniform than I did.

I've been in every stadium in the league, a few that don't exist anymore, a couple that were used just *one* time by NFL teams. I played in the old Metropolitan in Minneapolis, against the New York Jets in Shea Stadium many times, Busch Stadium in St. Louis, Baltimore Memorial Stadium. I went against the Raiders in Oakland, against the Rams in Anaheim, and played in the Rose Bowl. I saw action against the New Orleans Saints at Tulane Stadium before they had the Super Dome, and later I played there, too. I played in two other collegiate stadiums as a pro. In 1974, I was at Rice Stadium in Houston in the Super Bowl against Minnesota. I was also in the Super Bowl against the 49ers in Stanford Stadium in Palo Alto.

I always liked the older places: the Orange Bowl, Memorial Stadium in Baltimore, Cleveland, Chicago. They have an atmosphere to them. That was the way football used to be played, gladiatorlike—you felt like you were sitting in the Colosseum in Rome. Intimate, close to the action. In a lot of the newer places much of that intimacy is lost. In Joe Robbie Stadium in Miami, for instance, there is twenty to twenty-five yards from the bench to the stands because the place is also structured for baseball—room was left for foul lines and bullpens.

The indoor domed places without weather change and with air conditioning make for a sterile setting. People sit in a skybox on cushioned club seats, and they lounge back and order cocktails. It's like the theater or something, not like a football game.

Each city and stadium is like another country. I've never known Tampa to be really a vocal place. In

Atlanta, there aren't enough tickets sold for it to be noisy. The domed stadiums in Seattle and Minneapolis are very loud, but not all of the domes are like that. Houston you wouldn't consider a really viciously loud place.

But all stadiums have their own particular kind of mood, noise, and fans. Baltimore was called the "Asylum on 33rd Street" and for good reason. There and in the Orange Bowl the dimensions were such that you felt the fans right on top of you. The Meadowlands where the Jets and Giants play can get very loud. Fans give their arms a good workout, too. I can remember coins and stuff flying out of the stands. A place that gets loud and is known for its "dog pound" is Cleveland. I've got a lot more on that later on in the book.

Denver and Washington are sell-out cities. You have to be in somebody's will to get tickets for the Broncos. Mile High Stadium is loud, but the fans are not right on top of the field. And there's something about the thin air—the noise travels away very quickly. But there's so much hoopla, so much orange and blue in the stands and on the field, that it all makes Denver a pretty impressive place.

In Washington, RFK Stadium only holds about 55,000 people. Those fans there are in line for ten or twelve years waiting for season tickets. Those tickets are so rare that car dealers will give players cars to drive around in for the year just to get them. That's how they barter for tickets. It seems that everybody on the Redskins drives a brand new car.

Busch Stadium was pretty calm, and I don't remember KC as ever being real vocal. Playing against the

Patriots in Foxboro could get a little wild; the New England–Miami rivalry was a great one. The fans are close to you there, but it's an open-air stadium and the sound travels pretty good. I wouldn't consider it one of the louder places we played in. Three Rivers Stadium in Pittsburgh sells out all the time. There is something about those stadiums, like Three Rivers, outdoors in the cold that makes the noise carry better than in other places. You hated to go up to Pittsburgh and play in their "yard," as it was called. The turf there was hard, and when you were knocked down onto it, it was like falling on concrete.

A lot of teams had bands in stadiums that caused problems. After time-outs, they might still be finishing a tune for a few seconds which was annoying and very, very loud. And there were scoreboards in some places that were disconcerting, as in Houston where the fireworks would go off and annoy the hell out of you.

Night games in Dallas featured huge bugs that looked like cockroaches that fell through the hole in the roof out of the sky. But Dallas was never a loud place to play in. They were kind of sit-back fans there—used to winning. I played in Phoenix, and it was hotter than Miami: 96 degrees in November. We left Cleveland to play in Phoenix, and it was like going from a refrigerator into a furnace.

In all of those stadiums, I probably put on and took off as much eye black, heard more versions of "The Star-Spangled Banner," checked out more cheerleaders, took more plane rides, said as many Lord's Prayers, listened to more clubhouse pep talks, viewed more game films, than any other football player who ever lived. I survived three strikes, vicious linebacker shots, political intrigue, and changing styles in the NFL.

Along the way I met a lot of truly nice people, oddballs, and also some outright nasty characters. I'll tell you about a lot of them.

I always thought of myself as the layman quarterback, living out the dream of all those guys who played football in high school and college and now work in the steel mill or teach school or work on Wall Street.

A lot of nice things have been said about me, like sportswriter Mickey Herskowitz's comment: "If anyone ever erects a Hall of Fame for backup quarterbacks, the statue of Don Strock would be at the front of the rotunda."

I also got my share of jibes, like "Don's arm is very fresh. He hasn't thrown that many passes in his National Football League career." Actually, I threw enough to win 16 of the 22 games I started. That stat gave me a .727 percentage and made me, going into the 1990 season, the career percentage leader of all active NFL quarterbacks. Believe me, I was surprised myself to learn that.

I am ranked in the top five as one of the least-sacked quarterbacks ever. But in the 40-yard dash, they timed me with a sundial. And Rick Weaver, the voice of the Miami Dolphins forever, said: "When Don Strock runs, he looks like a flamingo in heat." So my not being sacked too much didn't come from my God-given speed or agility. It came from my feel for the time and the place and the circumstances on the field. There's more to playing football than athleticism. I'll get into all of that later on, too.

Some of the football writers called me the "Avis of Quarterbacks." One guy termed me the "Strock of Gibraltar," who always knew his place. Others referred to me as "Eveready." A few billed me as the "Goose Gossage of Football" and the "ultimate backup."

Some might see all of that commentary as put-down, but to my way of thinking it was the ultimate compliment—like being one of the best all-time relief pitchers in baseball.

I thought what I did was important to the success of my team and that I and all the other backups past and present play a very important role. It's like Mike Lynn, the former Viking general manager who went on to become president of the World League of American Football, said: "The most important position on a team is the quarterback, and the second most important position might be the backup quarterback."

But football is a game of injuries, and any guy playing the quarterback position is vulnerable, very vulnerable. Quarterbacks today wear a whole lot more protection than when I started the game, but they're still under-protected as compared with the guys going after them. They can't wear big shoulder pads because they need the flexibility to throw the ball. Out on the field there is never fear of getting hit because so much is going on; there's so much adrenaline flowing. I took hits lots of times. You don't realize you've taken those licks until you're in the shower and you see the bruises and feel them. Four or five times in my career I was wobbly. It's like you are gonged. You fade in and fade out.

The harsh truth is that no team can really count on a quarterback being there game after game throughout a season. That's just one of the reasons why backup quarterbacks are crucial. In 1988 and 1989 only six quarterbacks started all games for one whole season, and only Dan Marino and Randall Cunningham started every game both seasons.

The backup quarterback is usually the most popular guy on the team. Out there on the 50-yard-line he's there in the stadium helping in the play calling, encouraging his teammates, praising them for a good play, slapping them on the rump, and offering sympathy for a mistake.

At the same time the backup is there, at least I was there, prepared to get into the game at any time from the first snap to the final play. Each week I'd prepare myself for action, knowing that I was one play away from being out on the field quarterbacking the team.

Whenever things are going good, the quarterback gets too much credit, and when they're going bad, he gets most of the blame. That goes with the job. Another thing that goes with the job is that when things are going bad for a football team the fans start screaming: "We want ————." That's great for the ego. The only problem is when the fans' chanting "We want ————" changes to the coach saying "————, get in there and take over," and the backup isn't ready—that's not so great for the ego. And that happens an awful lot of the time.

Just that happened in 1978. Baltimore and Cincinnati were favored teams to make the play-offs. Bert Jones of the Colts and Kenny Anderson of the Bengals were both injured. Their backups took over: the Colts went 0–7; the Bengals went 1–6. I also took over that season—for Bob Griese when he got hurt—and won five of the seven games I started, which helped us tie for first place in our conference. That's the story on what can happen when you have a backup ready to play and others who are not ready.

There's a much different mentality that operates on the part of a starter and a backup. The starter begins the game with a clean slate with what he feels are his best twenty passing plays. He knows he is starting and feels that he is finishing. That's the mind-set. On the other hand, the backup never knows if and when he is going to be in a game. If he comes in and his team is ahead, he is going to run traps and stuff to try to let the clock run out. He's not going to throw the ball down the field. If he comes in when his team is behind, the backup has to do whatever is necessary to move his team down the field to try to get seven points. And when seven may not be the winner, he has to line up again and do it again, and maybe again.

We'd go into games with maybe 150 plays in the game plan, and I'd cut the list to 60 in my own personal game plan even before the game started, just because there are only 65 or 70 offensive plays run in a game by each team. Having a list of 150 is not necessary. There are also a lot of repeat plays. So I could never fully understand why there were 150 plays for everyone on offense to learn.

It seems like a tough thing to do, to master all the numbers and remember who goes where and why. But what helped was the codes we had set up, the repetition, and the practice.

The teens—18, 19, any running play that started with

a one—were set up for the fullback to carry the ball. Plays that started with a three in the huddle call were designed for the halfback to carry the ball—like 19 straight flow 38! In play action if the play starts with a three, as in pass 338, that would be a bootleg pass. If the play started with a five, as in 538, it would be a type of option screen pass or a regular screen pass.

As the game would wear on, if I was calling the plays from the sidelines, I'd be weeding those plays out that wouldn't be useful because of the time left in the game or the score. If I came into the game and we were ahead by 14 or 21 points, I might run plays to show them off to the following week's opposing team. That would make them think: oh, they do run that trap inside on third down. They do run that flow 38 on third down. They do run the quick hitch on first down. We haven't seen that.

It was a kind of false advertising, thinking a game or two ahead. But it was all part of the chess game, the game within the game that takes place every week in the National Football League. I'll get into more of this later on in the book—all the good inside stuff.

In general, there are two kinds of backups—those on the way up and those on the way down. The 1990 season saw the backup quarterback rosters filled with the guys who seemed to me not quite ready to play on a regular basis like Washington's Stan Humphries, Rich Gannon of Minnesota, Seattle's Kelly Stouffer, Andre Ware of Detroit. And, of course, Jeff Hostetler—and you know what happened to him! And then there were the guys who were former starters who were downgraded, sent to the bullpen: Chuck Long of the Rams, Marc Wilson of the Patriots, Philadelphia's Jim McMahon, San Francisco's Steve Young, Tony Eason of the Jets.

I'm sure there's a lot of frustration with those former starters. Guys who have been number one all through the years have to struggle with the frustration of not starting.

I was there in a different category. My position was backup except for a couple of years when I shared the quarterbacking duties with another player. I was there like an insurance policy through almost two decades.

You never want to be the backup, but the opportunity for me to be more than that didn't really come along. When I began my career in the NFL with the Miami Dolphins, Richard Nixon was president, Don Shula's son David was 12 years old and a ball boy, and Bob Griese was the main man at quarterback and in his prime. In between was David Woodley, who started with Shula calling the plays. When things weren't working out for David, I would be put into the game. After that Dan Marino came along. When Dan came in, I was in my eleventh year, and my role was "You're developing this guy to come in and play."

So I was there on the Dolphins behind two guys—one who was admitted to the Pro Football Hall of Fame in 1990 and the other who is pretty sure to go in someday, too. And when I played for the Cleveland Browns, I was there as a backup behind Bernie Kosar, one of the top quarterbacks in the game.

There are some things you'd love to change. You'd love to be the starter for seventeen years. But that opportunity arises for only a certain few. On the other hand, the opportunity to just be a quarterback on an NFL team exists for very few. If every team carried three quarterbacks, which they don't, there'd be just eighty-four people in the world any given year who would be NFL quarterbacks. So I take some pride in that—in surviving for seventeen years as one of that elite group.

There were times when I was discontented and when I knew that other teams were interested in having me as their starter. "Go ahead," Don Shula, the Miami coach would say. "Try and make a deal for yourself and we'll see if we can get it done." There were deals that were always pending, but somehow they could never get done. So the years moved along. In a blink of an eye, it seemed, I went from the young and future starter to the reliable old veteran....

Very few can leave a job in the financial shape NFL players wind up in. A guy who only plays two years gets severance pay of $5,000. Those who play four years leave the game with $70,000. My severance was $150,000 and the opportunity to collect a pension at age 45. That's the fat side if you last seventeen years. On the lean side is the cold fact that the average player lasts just 3.6, 3.7 years.

The only thing people see is the game on Sunday, but they don't know what you have to go through to get there. That's another thing this book will talk about. I survived, but not totally unscathed. I had ankle surgery and still creak a little bit when I walk around. My ankle twitches at the oddest times. My hands are in semi-good shape, but I have scars on them from getting them banged by helmets and sometimes my wrist aches

when I golf or move it normally. Others were not so
lucky. They carry around the scars and the strain every
day of their life of being banged around. Dan Hampton
is known as Danimal. He had more than 300 stitches,
15 broken bones, 10 knee surgeries. Larry Csonka gave
better than he got, but he still had many broken noses
and bruises. Tony Dorsett was all finesse, but at his
weight running the ball for all those years, he has to be
hurting every time he gets out of bed in the morning.
Earl Campbell, for sure, feels the price he paid as a
running back. Jim Otto has replacement knees. Joe
Namath walks around with a limp and needs a plastic
knee replacement.

As for me, all I know is that I can still carry out the
garbage and that I'm thrilled to be in the shape I'm in.
As for being retired from the game...coaching...an-
nouncing...scouting...that remains to be seen.

FROM WARWICK TO VIRGINIA TECH

THE beginning was almost noon, November 27, 1950. My mother's name is Mabel Irene Pierce Strock. My father's name is David James Strock, Sr., out of Pennsylvania Dutch and German stock. My mother is Irish and English. My brother is David James Strock, Jr., and my sister is Deborah Jo. We are all DJS, except my mother who is MIP, which is most important person.

Our first house was in St. Peters, Pennsylvania, near Pottstown. My father's father hauled coal that they took out of the mines, and my mother's dad was a logger. He had his own business and cut down trees for lumber, telephone poles, and caskets.

Both my mother and father had athletic backgrounds. She was a very good basketball player in the 1940s, as was my father, but baseball was his real strength. His nickname was "Rip" because he was a big home run hitter. In fact, when he was 24 years old, the St. Louis Cardinals wanted him to go into their minor league system. But my dad already had two sons and family responsibilities, so that was not to be.

I grew up in Warwick, Pennsylvania, in a house that my father built from scratch with his own hands with two of his friends. We moved into it in 1953. My dad's main job was at Grace Mines, a subsidiary of the Bethlehem Steel Company. He also worked at a granite quarry, where he cut tombstones by hand and shaped and polished them. He also built houses—three jobs a day just to make ends meet.

Dad would come home with soot and grime on his work clothes. He'd get out of those clothes and have a couple of beers before dinner. Then when the food was put out, he'd usually take whatever he wanted first, and after that, we'd go after it. We had some of the best bread and cream-filled doughnuts, which we bought from the Amish. We ate scrapple and homemade sausage.

Warwick is near Reading and Phoenixville, about forty miles from Philadelphia. It's in the Pennsylvania Dutch country, wonderful farm country. The Amish drive around in their horse-drawn buggies; the Mennonites drive all-black cars—even the bumpers are black. My family attended Pine Swamp Evangelistic Church.

There were about 250 people in my hometown, and I knew every one of them. Warwick had no sidewalks, no movie theater. The one we all went to was in Pottstown, eight to ten miles away.

But for a kid growing up, it was a tremendous place to be. There were a lot of country fairs, especially in the summer. It was a slow-paced life where we had a lot of good times.

When I was in junior high, I even had fun planting tobacco for a farmer for fifty cents an hour. I'd sit on the back of a plow with a little pump in front of me that shot water and insecticide and stick the plant in the hole as the plow moved along. I'd get pretty dirty by the time the day's work was done, but that was part of the deal. Bailing hay, working on combines, mowing lawns—all of that made up my odd jobs growing up.

My father was a big hunter. At one point, he and eight other guys bought a cabin up in Renova, Pennsylvania, near the New York State line. He was a tremendous deer-hunter, a heck of a shot. My mother used to cook venison steak or venison roast for my friends when they came up before basketball games for dinner. It would be our pregame meal. We had a pool table in the basement, and we'd play after dinner and then we'd go to the game.

My brother David is two years older than me, and we were always very competitive with each other in sports. When we were in Little League, my mom used to make us take a nap before our games. I guess that helped because we were both all-star players in the league.

In my growing up years, sports was a consuming thing for me. I read the *Pottstown Mercury,* one of the all-time great newspapers. And the *Philadelphia Evening Bulletin,* which is no longer in existence. To this day, the first thing I look at is the sports page.

I was a big fan of the Philadelphia Eagles and still check them out. When I was nine years old in 1960 they won the title behind Norm Van Brocklin at quarterback. The game was at Franklin Field against the Green Bay Packers. Few people recall that Van Brocklin's backup was Sonny Jurgenson. I always took note of everything back then—even backups.

We had a black and white television set. My father and I would sit on the couch on a Saturday afternoon and watch the Phillies play a doubleheader. The players that I remember from that time were Johnny Callison, Richie Allen, Don Demeter, Chris Short, Jim Bunning. My father would drink several beers—Reading, Schmidts of Philadelphia, Schaefer—and we'd talk baseball.

I listened to the game on radio when Wilt Chamberlain, who was from the Philadelphia area, scored a hundred points against the New York Knicks. When I was in the seventh grade our class went to a game. Chamberlain was walking around on the court before the game started. I was probably about five feet eight. He was seven feet one inch, and the biggest, strongest man I've ever seen in my life.

In the ninth grade I was about five feet ten. But when I started my sophomore year in high school I was almost six four. So I had a very growing summer.

My high school, Owen J. Roberts, was small. Just 258 graduated in my senior class, and that was the largest they had there in a long time. There were only two blacks in the whole school. Most of the kids that went there had parents and grandparents who had gone through the same route. So there was a real continuity. The whole school came out of only seven different townships—St. Vincent township, Warwick township, and so on.

I lettered in baseball, football, basketball, and track. I jumped center and played guard for the basketball team. When the football season ended, we had basketball practice the following day. In my junior year, I distinctly remember playing in the first basketball game of the season just three days after the football season was over and scoring 40 points.

My family was a great rooting section; they went to almost all of my games—except for my father, who couldn't make a lot of football games because he worked on weekends. As a matter of fact he didn't care if I played football. He had played a lot of soccer, but he didn't really understand football all that well. He certainly does now, though.

In one basketball game, we were getting beat pretty good. I had already scored my 22 points or whatever, and I wasn't really hustling. Driving home with my dad he said: "You know you have tremendous ability. You're head and shoulders above the guys you're playing with. But you played below them tonight, and if you don't want to be out there, and you're not going to hustle and you're not going to give your best, then give some poor guy on the bench who would love to be in the game the chance to play, because you didn't even try tonight." That little lecture had the biggest effect on me.

The drugs, counterculture thing was just getting under way across America when I was a high-school student. And the Vietnam War was heating up. I was in the middle of all of that, but it didn't affect me a whole lot or the hometown people. Except that a lot weren't crazy about the war and all the casualties. Many of them were vets from WWII. But there wasn't a whole lot of local debate about the war. We had a very patriotic community, a close-knit community with a lot of Elks Clubs, Owls, Moose, American Legion.

In my sophomore year I wasn't given much playing

time. One of the coaches said that I was a hood who smoked cigarettes and spent too much time hanging out with the boys and that kind of stuff. But that was just a phase that I got over fast.

In my junior year I was back into sports. I was a pretty good pitcher in American Legion ball and helped out team finish third in the state. The Detroit Tigers wanted me to play in their organization. But at that point, I was sixteen years old. It was kind of the reverse of what happened to my father. He was too old with too many responsibilities for the Cardinals; I was too young for the Tigers.

The last half of my junior year I was the starting quarterback for our high-school team, and we beat our big arch rival, Pottstown High School, in the Thanksgiving Day Game. That was what everybody lived for the whole year. We could be 0–9 and line up and beat them and our year would be successful. I know that kind of rivalry exists still in small towns all over America.

One image that stands out from that time is a quarterback named King Corcoran, who played on the minor-league Pottstown Firebirds. That team would ride to the 7,000-seat stadium on a bus. But Corcoran would be right behind in his Continental, and he'd pat old ladies on the fanny and actually "moon" the crowd.

I was semitough but shy as a high-school kid. And I remember how I was turned off by that kind of showboating. For me, playing the game was enjoyment, but not flaunting yourself.

I was big on learning all the ins and outs of any game that I played. On the football field we ran the I formation. We ran the split formation. We did a lot of stuff that people are using today. My high-school coach was Henry Bernat, who just retired. My brother, who is the athletic director at Owen J. Roberts High School, also played quarterback for Henry.

When I played for Henry, his job was sort of in jeopardy. He hadn't won in a while. But I was all-everything in my senior year and we tied for the title, and that kind of helped his job.

For me it was time to move on. Scholarship offers came in—from Penn Mil Academy, Villanova. I went up to Penn State for a visit and they would have taken me, but I wasn't crazy about the operation there. It was too big. I talked to Morehead State about basketball and was offered a scholarship by Wake Forest in basketball.

I wound up going to Virginia Tech because they played a major schedule and because of a fellow named John Devlin, who recruited me.

People always ask why I didn't wind up at a bigger football college. One of the reasons was that I made it known that I preferred to stay as close as possible to home. Virginia Tech, about 400 miles from my home, was closer than most. The college is in Blacksburg, about 40 miles south of Roanoke. It was a very close community. My freshman year, there were about 9,000 students, and a lot of them were ROTC. There were only 700 girls on campus, but Radford University was close by, and it was all women, so that helped things a little.

There were very few black students at Virginia Tech, whose fight song was "Dixie." That got dropped after my second or third year there.

It was an adjustment being away from home and

being in the South, and my dad still talks about how the day they dropped me off, they wanted to take me back with them.

I was there probably a week and said, "That's it, I'm out of here." I had my bags packed and I was ready to walk out the door. Then John Devlin, who had recruited me, came in. "Give it a chance, give it the opportunity, give it at least a year to see if you like it or not."

I stayed. There was never any money involved. Maybe fifteen dollars a month for laundry—that was it. But the education was free, and I made the most of it.

My first game for Virginia Tech we played in Birmingham, Alabama. On my first play I dropped back to pass and was forced to scramble and ran to the right into the sidelines. Boom! I ran right into Bear Bryant, the legend. I thought of the George Blanda line: "This must be what God looks like."

"Excuse me, sir," I said. I don't remember what he said, but I don't think he was too happy being bumped about by a rookie quarterback.

The head coach at Virginia Tech was Jerry Claiborne. He was a very religious man. When I was recruited, he picked us up and took us to church in Blacksburg, where he gave the sermon. He was also a very physical type who hated to lose. His practices were very demanding, and he prided himself on having a tough football team.

In my sophomore year I was red-shirted—on F Troop. That was a downer. The only real benefit in not playing football came because my brother had been awarded a scholarship and transferred to Virginia Tech, so that when I began my second year of playing football my brother was there with me. He was married and had a child, so we didn't room together, but we spent a lot of quality time together. He was the left-footed kicker and I was the holder.

In my junior year Coach Claiborne left Virginia Tech and was replaced by Charlie Coffey, who had come from Arkansas. The offensive coach was Dan Henning, now the head coach of the San Diego Chargers. Dan really set the tone and taught me about quarterbacking, huddle composure, attitude. We threw the ball around a lot—drop-back pocket passing.

I learned a lot, and in my junior year I was the leading passer in the country going into the last weekend—leading by 33 completions. But Brian Sipe threw for 34 completions and just beat me out.

In my senior year everything was going well for me and for Virginia Tech. My brother kicked the winning field goal against Oklahoma State, ranked at the time in the top 20 in the country. And we were *Sports Illustrated* players of the week together. I threw for 527 yards in the game against the University of Houston. Man, I was arm weary. Virginia Tech was 4–7 in my junior year—they had been rebuilding for years. We went 6–4–1 my senior year, and for Virginia Tech that was unbelievable. I was the top collegiate passer and total offense leader and set 28 records at Virginia Tech—most of them in passing. That was unbelievable, too.

But when my college career came to an end, even with all my football accomplishments a matter of record I never considered being drafted by a National Football League team. Playing in the NFL didn't really seem like something I'd want to do. And it never even dawned on me that I had a chance to be drafted. Virginia Tech didn't have a lot of big-name players on its football team other than myself. We had no big football school recognition, so not that many scouts used to come around to see us play.

My brother and I ended up graduating from Virginia Tech together, sitting in the stands right next to each other. I graduated with a degree in distributive education and had taken courses that could lead into teaching.

But when I was invited to participate in postseason all-star games, I started thinking a little bit about the NFL. How could I not start thinking with all the prodding, probing, pushing going on.

There were the scouts for the pro teams who came around at those all-star games. They measured players, weighed us, gave us tests to see how smart we were. It was synonyms, antonyms, that kind of stuff. There were times I was taking three tests in one day. Blesto, a combine that represented about ten or eleven NFL teams, was really into evaluating players and had all kind of physical and mental tests. The whole thing got a bit bothersome.

But that was nothing compared with the agents. They were like vultures descending on their prey. The phone calls, the letters, the guys cornering you—it was a mess. I wasn't one of those players from a football factory, wasn't someone who had gotten a tremendous amount of publicity during my collegiate career. And I was being bothered and badgered a lot. I wondered what it must have been like for guys who were stars in major programs. It must have been impossible. There were guys handing out their cards and making all kinds of promises. It was like they were herding a bunch of animals.

I played in the Hula Bowl and did well. A day before I was scheduled to play in the Blue-Gray game, I was sick with the flu and a 102-degree temperature. This guy in a fancy suit from New York City, the agent for Bubba Smith at the time, just knocked on the door of my room and walked in. He had a quart of orange juice in his hand.

"How are you feeling?" he asked.

"Not too good," I said, making a face like "Why don't you just go out and be about your business and leave me alone?" But I could see this was a guy who wouldn't take a hint.

"Oh, that's too bad. But maybe some of the stuff I'm gonna show you will make you feel a hell of a lot better."

Then he opened up his attache case which had a little TV screen in it. Right there in my room he showed a video tape. It was all about what he could do as far as agent representation was concerned and things like that. You might say it was his own personal highlight film.

"What do you say?" he asked.

"Very impressive."

"I have another one to show."

"Some other time," I said.

"Now is the best time," he said.

"Later, please."

"Now is the best time."

"Not for me. Thanks for the visit. But at this point I don't know what I'm going to do with my life. Let me get back to you." As you probably guessed—I never got back to him. Talk about a pain in the ass.

I still had a touch of the flu but went out there and competed in the Blue-Gray Classic Game. I did very well and was voted the Offensive Player of the Game. Holding my own against people who were supposed to be the best in the collegiate game—and doing maybe better than most—started me thinking a little bit more about possibly playing in the NFL.

And then there was Mike Trope, a young guy then, just starting out as an agent, a year younger than me. He made me do some more thinking about agents, the pros, life after college. Mike called me up and, as I recall it, said, "I want to have three players in my stable: Johnny Rogers, the Heisman Trophy winner; Rich Glover, the Outland Trophy winner; and you, the leading passer. I'd like to fly you to LA, put you up in the Beverly Hilton, the whole nine yards. You'll have a good time and we'll see how we get along. What do you say?"

I said, "Yes." I couldn't say no. I had never been to Los Angeles, so at least I'd get that out of the deal if nothing else. Trope flew me out first class, picked me up in a limo. I even had a beer in the backseat. Man, I was living high.

We got to the room in the hotel. "Here's the contract," he said. "Just go ahead and sign it, and we'll just have a good time for a day or so."

"What's the contract all about?"

"Standard stuff."

I took a quick look: 7 percent of this, and 12 percent of that, and half of any NFL signing bonus I might get...and option clauses and a whole bunch of other things that didn't seem to be what I'd like to be bothered with.

"No, I can't sign..."

"Not to worry," he said. Then he ripped that contract up and said, "Well, let's talk about what we want to do."

And I said, "I don't know, this is kind of sudden here—you're making this move on me."

"Let's go to dinner," he gave me a half wink. "It's always better to talk about these things over a good meal." So we went to dinner at Trader Vic's. We had a nice dinner. He had some other ideas about representation. I didn't like those either. Finally, I managed to get him to drive me to the airport and flew back home. I was only in Los Angeles a few days, but it seemed like forever.

Back in Pennsylvania I thought I was safe. But Trope was persistent. I'll give him that. He was calling me at one or two in the morning my time from LA. My mother was answering the phone and getting a little annoyed with the whole deal.

"Why don't you just tell this guy yes or no?"

So I get on the phone and I say, "Mike, I don't think I can use your services."

He goes, "I'll tell you what I'm going to do. I'll do the first year for nothing."

And I say, "Now I KNOW I don't need your services," 'cause my father told me one time, "Anything that looks too good to be true, is." So that was it with Mike Trope. Later I read about how he had problems with other athletes like Earl Campbell and Tony Dorsett.

With all that happening, with agents phoning and writing and bothering me, I figured if I linked up with one, that would stop all the others. Virginia Tech graduate Johnny Oates, a catcher for the Philadelphia Phillies, was one of the first players Jerry Kapstein represented. Johnny recommended me to Jerry, who was 28 years old at the time.

So I called him up and said, "Let's meet for lunch." From that lunch to today, Jerry has been my agent. Not only is he one of the best in the business, even better he's a very special friend.

As the time of the NFL draft came closer, all the top college players had things said about them—some good and some bad. The bad things sometimes can be the kiss of death. I got mine from Abe Gibron, then the head coach of the Chicago Bears. An outspoken kind of guy, Gibron came out in the newspapers and said that at 202 pounds I was physically not strong enough to take the pounding in the NFL. That hurt me. It really did.

Gibron and some of the other NFL experts saw 6 feet 5 inches, 202 pounds, listed on the Virginia Tech stat sheets. And nobody checked to see how much I actually weighed. I played at between 208 and 210 in my senior year. And their thinking that I was not durable was bullshit. The only injury I suffered was a dislocated thumb. I popped the thumb back in on the sidelines and missed just one play in two years.

But I had those stereotypes hanging over me when I was invited to a banquet at the Columbus, Ohio, Touchdown Club where I was honored as the best collegiate passer of the year.

In the Celebrity Lounge people were hanging around, talking, having cocktails. I happened to spot Don Shula, the coach of the Miami Dolphins.

I walked up to him. "You know, if you're looking for a quarterback, I'll be available."

He goes, "Yeah, you're a lot bigger than they say you are. You know, Earl Morrall is in his eighteenth year. We may be looking for somebody. You might like the weather in the winter in Miami."

Sure, I was thinking, all Miami needs is another quarterback. All they had going for them was two guys named Bob Griese and Earl Morrall, two guys who would probably wind up in the Hall of Fame. And the Dolphins just finished a 17–0 season—they sure needed help.

Back in 1973 the professional drafts weren't like they are today, filled with national television exposure, all the hype and hoopla. Most players just waited by the phone.

I was waiting by the phone around midnight the end of the first day of the NFL draft. A lot of clubs had sent me a little slip asking where I'd be the day of the draft. I had filled it out and mailed it back to them. The Miami Dolphins never sent me a questionnaire while I was in college, never sent me a slip to know where I'd be on draft day. I had that conversation with Shula, but I thought of that as a joke.

The phone rang. I picked it up on the second ring. I didn't want to appear too anxious. The guy on the other end was Les Miller, a scout.

"Congratulations, Don, the Miami Dolphins just drafted you."

I was in shock.

Then Don Shula came on the phone. "I liked what I saw at the Columbus Touchdown Club, and we think you can help us. Welcome to the Miami Dolphins."

THE
EARLY YEARS:
1973-1976

I WAS drafted in the fifth round by Miami, the 111th player taken, the seventh quarterback. Others in the class of '73 included Bert Jones of LSU, Ron Jaworski of Youngstown State, Joe Ferguson out of Arkansas, Dan Fouts from Oregon. Abe Gibron signed Gary Huff of Florida State, but Gary didn't play in the league that many years.

My contract called for $20,000, $24,000, $28,000, over the first three years. I got a $15,500 up-front signing bonus and $4,750 bonuses after the third preseason game for two years. So the total deal came to $97,000. I was making more money than I ever dreamed of and paid more taxes on what I made the first year in the NFL than my mother and father made together in salary. I was even a little reluctant to mention to them how much I was making.

Fortunately, I didn't fall into the same trap that many young players experience. I spent money, but I didn't go crazy about it. I was always a blue jeans and sneakers guy, but I went out and got some nice clothes.

29

I also splurged and bought myself a Lincoln Town Car, white with a blue leather interior.

All my friends and relatives were impressed that I was going to be with the Dolphins. But Miami had just come off a 17-0 season, and everyone wondered, especially me, what my chances of making good in Miami were. I was prepared to give it all I had, knowing I could wind up with some big disappointment.

I drove down from Pennsylvania for the first mini-camp in May with a girl friend of mine. I had never been to Miami before in my life. The air was soft and warm, and with the ocean and people on vacation, the town really did have that resort feeling everyone said it was famous for.

Don Shula was in his tenth year as an NFL head coach then. He was a fixture not only in Miami but throughout the National Football League. His pro football career began with the Cleveland Browns as a defensive back way back in 1951—I was one year old them. In 1963, Shula succeeded Weeb Ewbank as head coach of the Baltimore Colts. How Shula came to the Dolphins is still a subject of some speculation. As the story goes, Alabama coach Bear Bryant flew to Miami after the 1969 season to meet with Joe Robbie, a part-owner of the team, and Danny Thomas, the majority owner of the team. They were set to discuss giving the Bear the head coaching spot on the Dolphins. But it never came to be.

Baltimore had suffered an upset loss to the New York Jets in Super Bowl III in 1969. That was the game where Joe Willie Namath put his money where his mouth was—he guaranteed the Jets would win that game and that's just what they did. The next thing everybody knew was that on February 18, 1970, Shula became head coach of the Miami Dolphins.

Although what really happened is still unclear, it looked to me that something odd did happen. Why would Shula leave Baltimore after posting a seven-year record of 71–23–4 and taking the Colts to two NFL championships games and come to Miami—a franchise that to that point had never had any success? One line of talk was the one Baltimore's Tom Matte, one of the best players in Colt history, told me. The Dolphins hadn't won anything, but they were young and had promise. Some of the stars on the Colts were getting older, well into their thirties. But something went on. The word some used was "tampering." Whatever it was, NFL Commissioner Pete Rozelle gave the Dolphins' number one pick to Baltimore in 1971. Was that compensation for losing Shula? Very few know for sure. I feel that I can safely say it was the best number one pick the Dolphins ever had. And that includes the likes of Bob Griese, Dan Marino, and Larry Csonka.

Joe Robbie was a very tough businessman, a guy you loved to hate. Not too many people on the team had much of a relationship with him. The only time he was on the field was on team day to get his picture taken. But in the community, he was very oriented to charity.

A man who made his money from the Miami Dolphins, not like a lot of the other owners who have outside interests, Robbie always looked to save each and every penny. The division of him taking care of the business aspects of the Dolphins and Shula minding the football end was a perfect setup—it was unique in the NFL. And that was one of the major reasons for the success of the franchise—each man taking good care of his own turf.

They worked well as business associates, but Shula and Robbie were not the closest of friends. There was one team banquet where they almost came to blows, and they would have had not the priest who traveled with us broken it up. There were also other incidents between them.

Don Shula was very businesslike, a man who didn't want anything to be lax. There was a sign in the clubhouse meeting room: THE WINNING EDGE. The first "E" stood for enthusiasm. The "D" was for desire. The "G" was for gassers, which we ran—sprints. And the last "E" was for extra study.

All kinds of opinions have been expressed about Don Shula. I especially like what Nat Moore said: "Don Shula as a coach is one of the best in the game from Monday to Saturday. But on Sunday he's average."

There was a linebacker named Kevin Reilly from Villanova who came to the Dolphins at about the same time as I did. We were starting to become friendly with each other. But he was released. That was a quick first lesson about the nature of the beast that is pro football. In college you made friends with guys and stayed friends with them for four years. In the pros you would start to make friends, and many times they'd be gone before you had a chance to even really get to know them.

It's the dream of millions of guys in the United States to play in the National Football League. Very, very few make it. Those that do get drafted and show up at the training camps are kind of meat on the hoof to be measured, weighed, tested, probed, inspected, second-guessed, sized up, what have you.

The ones that make it to the camps even for a cup of coffee are good, real good. They have been great stars in high school, college. But in the NFL it's a different story.

Those that have made the Dolphins through the years are listed in their media guide in dark print. The others are, too, but in lighter typeface, never making the team.

Generally, the veterans don't come into camp until after the first week or ten days. So some of the draft picks I never met or even saw. They're phantoms—just names in light print.

At the start, all the hopefuls stay at St. Thomas University near Miami in a barrackslike arrangement. Then the club helps them find lodgings for them if they make the team. It was amazing for me to see the different kinds of personalities that made their way to the Miami Dolphins through my fifteen years there. Guys drafted very low and making $50,000 a year came in driving $35,000 cars. And there were others who came in beat-up vans or old cars or got driven down and dropped off by their parents. Some of the first-round picks were anxious to show off their signing bonus and big pay-checks and they had expensive foreign cars, stereos, TVs, whatever they could buy—they flaunted the stuff.

There were always people hanging around with deals, always women in the background, always ways young guys could get into trouble. Some steps were taken to keep players protected. My first or second year on the team, league security came down with a sheet six pages long of places players could and could not go. Surprisingly, one of the off-limits places was one of Richard Nixon's favorite eating spots. I guess it was off-limits because the president went there.

Every guy who came to the Dolphins with a hope and a prayer had a story. Some had real happy endings, but there was a lot of sadness, broken hearts, real tragedy, too. I'll take you through some of those drafts as I go along and talk about some of the guys. A lot of them I'm sure you'll remember.

The number 17 and last pick of Miami in the 1973 draft was Charley Wade, a wide receiver from Tennessee State. A small guy, very fast, Charley always had a gun with him for "personal" purposes, whatever.

Carl Taseff, one of the assistant coaches, and Don Shula have been buddies since high school. Carl was call "the Turk," because it was his job to bring players the news that they were cut. Some said that Carl had a tough time acting out that role, but sometimes I think he might have really enjoyed it.

Well, he was doing his job when he knocked on Charlie Wade's door to bring him the news and have him return the playbook. But when the door opened, the sight that confronted Carl was Charlie Wade—gun in his hand. As the story goes Carl broke the news and broke away even faster.

We had a seven- or eight-week camp when I first came in, and we played six games. I played in a preseason game against Dick Butkus in his last year. He had a bad knee at the time (and he wound up suing the Chicago Bears for not providing proper medical and hospital care after a disabling knee injury and settled lawsuit out of court). Kind of pigeon-toed on that one leg, Dick was used as a fullback on the punt teams, so he was the guy who called the signals. Our guy returned a punt, and Butkus right in front of our bench just hammered him. Probably a little late, probably a little vicious.

Shula yelled at him: "Nice cheap shot, Butkus!"

Butkus turned around. He was sweating, and he had shit in his mustache and dirt all over his uniform. And he said, "Fuck you, Shula!"

Shula backed up a little, smiled, and gave him the line: "Hey, Dick, how you doing?"

Butkus was just the fiercest, fiercest competitor. It was a shame to watch him hobbling around in that state. I think he was in only his ninth year. He could have played many more years. It was sad to see what had happened to such a tremendous football player. I learned something from that—how the sport chewed guys up.

The Dolphins penciled me in as a backup behind Earl Morrall, Bob Griese, and Jim Del Gaizo, a left-handed guy, very vocal, from Boston who wanted the opportunity to play. There wasn't much chance for him, and Jim asked to be traded. They gave him his wish. Right at the end of the 1973 preseason he was sent to Green Bay.

After Jim was traded, things were a bit unsettled in my mind. I didn't know how the Turk worked—the guy I told you about who taps you on your shoulder and says: "Coach wants to see you."

I came into the clubhouse the day after the trade, the last cut day. I looked in my locker, and there's nothing there. No shoes, no helmet, no jersey, nothing. I'm sweating this out, sitting in my chair to collect myself.

Then I just got up and said, to nobody in particular: "I'm going in to see Coach Shula."

Everyone's head is down. I start walking down the hallway and three guys run back and stop me. Larry Csonka, Jim Kiick, and Larry Seiple.

"Hold on, Don," Csonka says. "We just wanted to jack around with you. We took all your shit." Then the three of them started laughing and pulling my things out of the hamper right next to where my locker was. I was had, but I was happy just to be there on the Dolphin depth chart behind Griese and Morrall.

In one of the first meetings I attended, Earl Morrall was talking to Don Shula about a game they had played in against each other back in 1956. I was six years old in 1956, the year Earl came into the league out of Michigan State. I listened to this talk and knew I was in fast company—the two of them had been around the pro game so long and Earl was closing in on 20,000 yards passing.

Players are superstitious about the numbers they wear. All through my college career I had worn number 15. Red Grange, when asked how he got number 77, replied: "The guy in front of me got number 76, the one in back got number 78."

My story of how I got number 10 on the Dolphins isn't as funny as the Red Grange line. Earl Morrall wore number 15 on the Dolphins, and I would have had a hell of a time getting it off his back. So they gave me number 10.

Earl had all that experience, a wealth of knowledge—a throwback with the black shoes and the short socks and the flat-top haircut. Just standing on the sidelines with Earl and watching him in games was a great learning process for me. I learned so much that it took a couple of years before I was able to package and put together all that I learned.

When I first came in, they gave quarterback tests that Shula made up. We'd go into his office to take them. I'd be sitting there grinding away. Earl Morrall and Bob Griese would finish in a few minutes and get restless seeing me killing their time. But they were nice about it.

Bob Griese was the thinking man's quarterback, the proven guy, while Earl was the veteran backup. Bob wasn't a real big guy, and he didn't have the strongest arm in the world, but he knew where to throw the ball, how to win. Bob had a great sense of the game—when to play-action, when not to throw. Those are the things you pick up if you watch, and I watched all the time.

Bob Griese had what they called a lazy eye, and he was the first football player to ever wear glasses, not goggles. He wore actual glasses. If it was raining or he got crap on them, he'd always have to take them off and clean them. During one preseason game they gave him something to take to combat this, and it didn't work. He wound up having a terrible time with double vision.

"Will you go in next series?" he asks me. "I'm having a hard time seeing out of my eye. It's a little blurry."

"Well, did you tell Coach Shula yet?"

"No."

All of a sudden there was a turnover and someone had to go in at quarterback. So I go running onto the field. Shula's looking for Bob, and he can't find him and he sees me running onto the field. On the very first play I threw a bomb and it was intercepted. Shula was speechless. A speechless Shula was something you didn't see too often, but you'll see what I mean later.

Bob drew up his own game plans, and from watching him I learned how to do it. Every Wednesday was offensive game practice. We had 150, 160 plays in the game plans. Every Wednesday night with Bob Griese's influence, I would cut it down to 50. Special situation plays, reverses, etc., brought it up to about 60. I learned a lot about coverages from Earl, what audibles to use in situations against different defensive coverages. Bob, Earl, and I were close. My first year with the team I was on what was known as a move squad, a two-man squad active during the week that could be deactivated on game day. Since I was the third quarterback, in practice I ended up by running other teams' offenses against our defense—"the No-Name Defense," given that nickname when Tom Landry said before Super Bowl VI that he couldn't name any of Miami's defensive players.

That was an experience—going against one of the best defenses ever assembled. It was difficult to complete a pass, just a chore to move the offense. I remember Nick Buoniconti, an undersized linebacker, a great player, telling me the "play's coming over here, here." He knew where plays were going before they were even run.

Larry Little was another player I had much respect for. Out of Bethune-Cookman College, Larry was born and raised in Miami and was big in town. They called him "Chicken" because he ate buckets of the stuff, but he wasn't Chicken Little by any means. Larry was a team leader, a captain and one of the first great pulling guards. He's not there, but he deserves to be in the Pro Football Hall of Fame.

I was told that I was going to spend my rookie season totally on the move squad, not in uniform. That didn't make me too happy, but I was just thrilled to be there on the Dolphins in all the quarterback meetings and involved in everything. It was a great learning experience seeing the styles of different teams and especially quarterbacks.

We started off the 1973 season beating San Francisco in the first game of the year for our 18th win in a row. Then on September 23 we played Oakland at Cal Berkeley Stadium. There was some bitching that Al Davis had wet down the field to screw around with and slow down our running game. I'm not so sure that was what happened. But it might have.

Daryl Lamonica was the Raider starting quarterback then, with Kenny Stabler waiting in the wings to get his chance. (By the end of the year Kenny would take over, so there was a changing of the guard with the Raiders as there was with other teams.) Lamonica was a big strong guy who fit the Raider mold. Their placekicker was George Blanda, 46 years old in his 26th and last season. Man, he was older then than my father, older than the fathers of a bunch of guys playing in that game. George didn't look good in a uniform, but there was respect for him every minute he was out there on the football field.

The Raiders had a great game plan. Lamonica had the image of the Mad Bomber and could throw the ball as deep as anyone who ever played the game. But in that game he played for field position, ran the clock down, threw the ball underneath, picked us, picked us, and set up the field position for Blanda to kick field goals. We lost the game, 12–7.

When the streak was stopped, no one was happy, but there was so much talent and so much pride on the Dolphins that another one was started that went ten games in a row. Those were the glory years for the Dolphins. Can you imagine a team going 28–1 in one stretch?

The Dolphins in those days went into games expecting to win, knowing other teams had to beat them, knowing they wouldn't beat themselves. There were few turnovers. It was precision football anchored by the running of Jim Kiick, Larry Csonka, and Mercury Morris and the pass catching of Paul Warfield.

Kiick said: "Astro Turf never bothers Larry and me because we can't make ninety-degree turns. In fact, I don't think we move fast enough to slip."

They didn't move that fast, but with Kiick burrowing under guys, Larry blasting over guys, and Mercury sprinting by guys, it was punishing football when it had to be that way, finesse, too, when we needed it.

A lot of moments stand out from my rookie season. We played Pittsburgh on December 3. It was a Monday Night Game. Jefferson Street Joe Gilliam was the Steeler starting quarterback. Dick Anderson intercepted him for a touchdown. In fact, Anderson had four interceptions and two touchdowns. Joe Gilliam didn't play well. He had some problems, and it came out about a year or two later that Joe had some serious drug problems, so I always wondered about that game. Terry Bradshaw came in for Gilliam and finished the game and played from then on. That started off the great Steeler years.

One of my great favorite players was another Pennsylvania guy—Joe Willie Namath. And it was special for me to see him play in the flesh. We beat him and the Jets twice in 1973—31–3 in New York, 24–14 in Miami. In both games Shula wouldn't call the horses off. I can still hear him muttering: "I just don't trust that damn guy." The memory of that Super Bowl loss to the Jets and Joe Namath was always there.

In Baltimore on December 9, Shula surprised a lot of people by starting Earl Morrall at quarterback. He did that out of sentiment, because Earl was on the verge of throwing for 20,000 yards. It was a kind of homecoming for Earl back in Baltimore and it was a nice idea starting him, but it backfired. We lost the game—only the second loss of the season.

The team that impressed me the most in 1973 was Dallas. We had already clinched our division when we went to Texas Stadium to play them. The game was a pride thing. Don Shula against Tom Landry. Roger Staubach against Bob Griese. Calvin Hill against Larry Csonka. The Cowboys then had so many great players— Jethro Pugh, Bob Lilly, Mel Renfro, Chuck Howley. The game was a defensive struggle. We won 14–7.

What was so interesting about the Dolphins in my first couple of years there was that if an opponent was conservative and honed into defense, the Dolphins could adjust to that style of play, and if the game became wide open and the other team was trying to put a lot of points on the board, the Dolphins could adjust to that, too. Versatility—any kind of game that was needed—that was just part of the strength of Miami.

The atmosphere on the Dolphins was businesslike, like going out to work, like knowing you couldn't help but succeed. And that team worked. That was one of the reasons the Dolphins won a lot of games in the fourth quarter.

Miami was not only a team dominant in wins. It was dominant in scores. We beat teams by big scores, and didn't beat ourselves. For a long stretch there in the 1970s the Dolphins were the least-penalized team in the NFL.

We swept through the 1973 play-offs and went to Houston to practice for the Super Bowl, scheduled to be played at Rice Stadium against Minnesota. As part of the team's preparation, Bill Arnsparger, our defensive coordinator, told me that I was going to play the role of Viking quarterback Fran Tarkenton in the practices.

"Every time you're in the pocket," he said, "scramble, take off anywhere."

So that's what I did. As you all know, I was never a big speed guy, but I did know how to wiggle about a little. The No-Name Defense was chasing me and getting pissed off, chasing me all that week and getting pissed off. The guys bitched to Arnsparger, who told them: "If Don gets you tired, what's gonna happen to you when you come up against Fran Tarkenton?" Some of them kept quiet after that, but others kept complaining to me to stop wiggling so much.

The Vikings were doing a lot of complaining of their own. As the designated home team, we practiced at the

Oilers' complex a few blocks from our hotel. Minnesota had a twenty-minute bus ride to a field that was not state of the art. Actually it was a high-school stadium in Houston where coaches and players had one cramped room for changing clothes, whatever. "I don't think our players have seen anything like this since junior high school," Minnesota coach Bud Grant snapped. The snapping didn't do him any good, but it gave the media some pregame Super Bowl controversy to kick around. They love that kind of stuff.

Joe Willie Namath made the statement before the Super Bowl began: "If Miami gets the kickoff and scores on the opening drive, the game is over." We got the kickoff. We scored on the opening drive. And the game was over. The final score was Miami 24, Minnesota 7—the second straight Super Bowl win for Miami. What had been accomplished was impressive. The Dolphins had gone 34–2 in two seasons. Talk about your great teams.

The game's Most Valuable Player was Larry Csonka, who gained 145 yards on 33 carries in Super Bowl VIII. After the game ended, Larry was all smiles despite a black eye and a puffed-up nose. A few of the reporters asked him what happened to his face. "It was a cheap shot," he said, "but an honest cheap shot. The guy came right at me and threw an elbow right through my mask. I could see the game meant something to him."

The game always meant something to Larry Csonka, who was a machine on the football field. He just strapped it on and ran straight into people. Csonka weighed in at 237 and played around 250. He was thick, and he always ran very low to the ground. He had short strong strides, which is the sign of a power back. Csonk was certainly the toughest guy I ever played with—physically. He used to look for people to run over. Guys would try to get out of his way.

There was one play I'll never forget. Larry had five or six guys on his back. You couldn't even see him. You just saw this pile moving forward. It might have gone a couple of more yards, and then the pile just collapsed. I guess that image was what led to Chicago safety Doug Plank's comment: "One time I was trying to tackle Larry Csonka around the ankles, but he was carrying so many of our men, I was afraid I'd hit a teammate."

In uniform, charging around on the field, he was a mean-looking thing, but Larry had a good sense of humor. Having dinner with him I always noticed he ate pretty well and liked his Johnny Walker a lot. Both he and Jim Kiick liked Johnny Walker.

I always liked Jim, who was fond of having his beer, playing a little cards, listening to music. He wasn't a big guy, but he was a great player and just had the knack of catching balls out of the backfield.

The Dolphins were so successful, so glamorous, so popular then that they were the biggest thing going all over Florida, all over the football world. It caused some problems, too. Three or four of the guys on our team were impersonated by people throughout the country. Some wrote bad checks using the names of Dolphin players. Some falsified credit cards.

One of the more interesting incidents involved a guy in and around the Georgia area who was dating a woman and was actually engaged to be married to her—and she thought he was Jim Kiick. All the time they were going together the guy told her that he could only visit her certain days of the week. Monday was one of his big days. It just so happened that they were together one Monday and the guy made a big mistake and turned on the TV. The Dolphins and Jim Kiick were right there on the TV screen—Monday Night Football. The way the story came out, the guy was arrested and there was hell to pay. I don't know if he went to jail or anything like that, but it was a classic case of impersonation—the woman about to marry a guy she thought was Jim Kiick.

There were headlines about the Dolphins' off-the-field activity, major stories about on-the-field exploits. The Miami Dolphins of that time were such a strong group—the explosive offense, the great No-Name Defense, the Kiicks, Csonkas, Warfields, Morrises, Langers, Littles, Kuechenbergs—legends and lesser lights, but all distinct personalities.

Howard Twilley was the last of the original Dolphins, a guy who was a twelfth-round draft pick who signed an $80,000 bonus. That was when the Dolphins were in the American Football League at war with the NFL. Howard couldn't run that well, but he had the moves and played the game to the limit, and that's what made him such a great receiver. The thing about him was that he was always reading the *Wall Street Journal*. It paid off. Howard ended up owning some twenty Athlete's Foot stores and made out very well financially.

Bill Stanfill, with the Dolphins from 1969 to 1976, was another fine player out of Georgia. And he was also a character. A great defensive end, Bill could have a chew in, a dip, smoke a Camel straight, and drink a

Coke at the same time. Bill was born and raised in Georgia and was a good old country boy and a good friend. We used to go out and have beers with him and just enjoy listening to his twang.

The Orange Bowl was always packed back then, so it was quite a thing being there. They still had Poly Turf on the field, and it could get awful hot even for the Dolphin players, but we were more used to it than the opposition and that gave us a bit of an edge. I saw firsthand how the heat could melt the opposition. It was the season opener against the San Francisco 49ers, the very first game I ever played in the Orange Bowl. John Brodie was their starting quarterback. The on-the-field temperature with the old Poly Turf was 123 degrees. It was a sweat bath, and Brodie just couldn't hack it. He didn't even come out after half time. He couldn't finish the game, and they were beating us by seven points at the time. Steve Spurrier ended up playing the second half, and we came back and won the game. Not because of him, but we were on a roll at the time, and the heat just finally wore them down.

One constant in the Dolphin schedule is that the last games of the year are always heavily weighted toward home games. A look at the year-by-year schedule shows it clearly. Some say it's by chance, but it's more like by design. I'm not saying the cold-weather teams don't enjoy having the opportunity to come down to a place like Miami late in the year. If it's winter and snowing outside your house, wouldn't you like to be where it's warm and palm trees are waving in the breeze? But that hot weather certainly affects them. If affects everyone, but the Dolphins are used to it and work in it year round.

Most of the visiting teams did some strange things to try to combat the heat. One time the Colts came down and they ate bananas three days in a row because they are rich in potassium and that helps prevent leg cramps. They beat us and they thought that was the key. The Bears came down and they had a lot of guys on their offensive line who were heavy and bulky. They also went for the banana deal. I don't think three of their offensive linemen even finished the game. They had to put their second line in, and we ended up beating them pretty good. And that happened a lot to clubs that came down.

The Orange Bowl, with metal benches in some sections instead of seats, had some of the old-time football flavor. It was always my favorite place to play. Usually, the field conditions were very good. Fan support was very good. The "horrible hankies" were in vogue. They had been thought of by an announcer in Miami as a way for fans to get into the act. That was a sight—some 70,000 people waving white hankies. It annoyed the hell out of visiting teams. Then they went to aqua hankies. Many people still have those hankies to this day.

So with the heat and the crowd noise operating most of the time, the Miami Dolphins have always enjoyed a decided home-field edge.

During my first couple of years with the Dolphins, I was far from prime time. But I did manage to get a couple of endorsement deals. For a nominal fee I said nice things about a restaurant in the North Miami

Beach area. My picture and that of my wife, Debby, appeared on a TV commercial with the line: "When I go out for dinner, I enjoy eating at ————." A few days later, Coach Shula called me in.

"Somebody called me up and told me that restaurant you did an ad for has got some problems." I laughed at that, but Shula said: "Don, I'm serious."

The next day the shit really hit the fan. Local FBI agents, league officials, security people came down to the Dolphin camp and began quizzing me. An investigative crime reporter wanted to interview me. Some photographer took my picture as I was walking off the field huffing and puffing after doing wind sprints with an out-of-breath look on my face. That picture ended up on the front page of the *Miami News*.

Of course, the whole thing was innocent on my part, and no one ever brought any charges against the restaurant. But that experience taught me a lesson about how important it is to check out whomever I associated myself with. It was a lesson I learned early in my career, and I relayed that lesson to many other players.

There's a sign in all National Football League locker rooms that advises the players not to engage in gambling or associate with any gamblers. But in Florida, with horses, dogs, jai alai, lottery, and sometimes even cockfights, it's difficult to stay away from people who gamble.

Many times friends or acquaintances would ask, "How are the Dolphins going to do this week?"

"They're going to win," I'd say.

"Do you think they'll win by four?"

I'd answer, "If they win by one point that'll be good enough for me."

Sometimes I'd overhear conversations: "Well Pittsburgh won this week."

And I'd say, "No they didn't. They lost by seven."

"Yeah," the guy would say, "but I was getting seven and a half."

Conversations like that make you think of the Pete Axthelm line: "I can't stand to look at a team that hasn't beaten the spread and thinks it's won." It also reminds me of the line by Paul Hornung: "The toughest thing was to miss that extra point when the line was three."

One of the positive things in the National Football League is the guidance and protection made available to players. League security comes down to talk to the members of each team, and they make a point of telling the guys not to discuss injuries, game plans, any inside information about teams with strangers. That's one way an attempt is made to put a crimp on gamblers getting any kind of an edge. Also National Football League security personnel let the players know that they will check out any people that the players might do an endorsement for, enter into business with, make an appearance for. They tell the players it's in their interest to let security know about such involvements because if any problem comes up, the player's ass is on the line.

You can imagine how many calls NFL security gets: "I saw so and so gambling in a card game." "I saw so and so hanging out with this character," and so on.

———

In 1974, the Dolphins drafted Gary Valbuena out of Tennessee in the tenth round. They called Gary the "Cosmic Cowboy." He drove an orange Corvette and always wore black and a black cowboy hat. Gary had a great arm but, in my opinion, never took enough time to learn the game. He never made the team, and later signed with the World Football League.

That year Ken Dickerson out of Tuskegee, playing in a preseason game, had a head-on collision and broke his neck and had to be taken off on a stretcher. That ended his dream.

One of the classic Don Shula stories that went around the 1974 training camp was how he had tried to get away from the spotlight after we had won the Super Bowl. The word was that he took his family during the off-season to an out-of-the-way place in New England for a little rest and recuperation.

On a quiet weekday night Shula and his wife went to the local movie house to take in a flick. The place was pretty empty when they got there, but as soon as Shula and his wife headed down the aisle, applause started.

Shula raised his hand. "Thanks," he waved to a couple of people. "It was a great season for the Dolphins, we accomplished a lot."

Suddenly, the place became quiet. "What Super Bowl?" a guy asked. "What the hell you talking about? The only reason you got applause is that the damn projectionist said the movie wouldn't start until we had ten people in the joint. You and your wife make ten. Sit down and shut up."

Talk about humbling experiences. Yet, I don't know if

even that humbled him. He's not too humble a guy. In fact, one of his specialties has always seemed to be trying to humble others.

So much of Shula's personality came out when we were watching films. Hours and hours of it, the lights on, the lights off. There was always a rookie who turned the lights on and off. And there was this incident with a young veteran named Tom Drougas, whom Shula really got his rocks off on. Right in the middle of the film, Shula yelled: "Turn the lights on." That stopped the projector.

The lights came on and as I remember it Shula said something like: "Drougas, I'm scouring the waiver wire right now. As a matter of fact, we're looking for anybody that can do the job a hair better than you. And your ass is gone."

Then Shula turned around. "Lights out. Start the projector!"

There weren't that many guys around who would start with Shula, but Jake Scott, a free safety and a free spirit out of Georgia, was one of them. At a team meeting Shula announced that all the players were expected to be in attendance at a banquet.

As my memory serves me Jake yelled out loud enough for everyone to hear: "I won't be there!"

Shula glared at him. "Everybody will be at the banquet."

"I'm not going to be there."

"Everyone," Shula snapped, "will be at the banquet or they'll be fined five hundred dollars."

"I don't care what you fine me," Jake looked the man in the eye. "I'm not going."

And he didn't go either. And that was a big stink in the papers. They fined him. But for Jake Scott it was all worth it. He had made his point.

As the 1974 season got under way, I dressed for all the games. That's where the image a lot of people always remember me for, standing on the sidelines wearing the mesh baseball cap and the jacket, began. Nowadays all NFL backup quarterbacks wear the baseball cap and jacket, so I guess you could say I started a trend.

I first started doing it when Bob Griese was playing so he could see me when I gave hand signals for coverages. If Bob wanted to know what coverages the other team had been in on, say, first down, he'd look over and I'd tell him with hand signals. It started then and became my trademark—the cap, the jacket, the hand signals. As the years went on, I just kept doing it for all of the Miami quarterbacks. They could look over and see easily. I wore a different-colored jacket from the team uniform—but I had only two basic colors to choose from, orange or aqua. Naturally, the hat was for protection from the sun. The jacket was a light windbreaker type thing, unless we were playing in cold weather. I wore that because before every game I warmed up and sweated a lot and wanted to keep that body heat in. I had to be ready to come into a game at any time. The jacket and Miami Dolphins' cap came off only when I tossed the ball in pregame warm-ups or held for extra points and field-goal attempts. But it was amazing all the odd times and unusual circumstances that I did get into in games.

My "backup" outfit attracted a lot of attention on and off the field. Some businesses in Miami approached me and offered to pay me if I wore a cap with their logo on it. But the NFL has strict rules that mandate that all the players wear only club-issued paraphernalia, except shoes. You had to wear official Dolphin-colored sweatbands, caps, etc. So I had to turn down all those offers. Too bad, I could have made a nice piece of change, as many do, because commercialism is just part of the game.

The whole shoe deal is astonishing. I was hooked up at one point with a fellow from Brooks shoes. I signed a deal to wear these silver football shoes with a gray-colored bottom and was paid $10,000 a year. And I was a backup. You can figure out what the starters got. I had a deal at another time with Pony. They picked me because anyone looking at the Dolphin sidelines would see me—I was there so much of the time.

Shoe contracts are the NFL way. All types of players, from big stars to those just starting out, sign shoe contracts. Nowadays there's a funny side to that, too. The big thing is spats. Players, especially receivers and defensive backs, tape over the shoes all the way up. It's like they're taping their ankles in a second tape job. Some of these guys wear Pony shoes because they think they're better or more comfortable and then have the equipment guy put Adidas stripes over the tape. So quite a few players are getting paid by Adidas but they're actually wearing another brand.

On March 31, 1974, Paul Warfield, Larry Csonka, and Jim Kiick went to another "brand." They shocked everyone in the National Football League when they signed up with the World Football League, a rival league just starting up. They were offered a million dollars each, or something like that, which was a lot of money for that time. They came on TV and announced they were taking it, and I guess Joe Robbie, the Dolphin owner, never had a chance to match it. Then it became a bidding war with other players. Incidentally, I was the fifth guy drafted off Miami by the Philadelphia Bell. But I was under contract to the Dolphins, so that never really panned out.

Everyone in Miami was stunned that three players of that caliber would jump off the Dolphins, but it was the kind of deal those guys just couldn't turn down. Their defections caused immeasurable injury to our team's morale as we went into the 1974 season because they played that year, but they were lame ducks.

On November 3, I got into my first NFL game, a bit of running the clock out in a 42–7 win over Atlanta, whose head coach was Norm Van Brocklin. The irony of that situation was that he was the quarterback I watched in the championship game in 1960 back home on our little black and white TV set. The Dutchman, as he was called, was a feisty guy who smoked cigarettes on the sidelines and told his players to step on them and put them out. Even though I was just mopping up, being on the field in that game was something special for me.

We had a formation and Paul Warfield was in the game with me. I knew Atlanta had a blitz on, but I didn't check off. When we came to the sidelines, Paul said in that soft-spoken voice: "I know you would have checked off if the game was on the line."

"Sure," I said and I smiled.

He wasn't reprimanding me, but just letting me know

what the score was. Paul was just a super player, a guy who always knew what the score was. I threw to him in practice many times and just regret I never had the chance to do so in an official game. At his position, Paul was the best who ever played the game. Very business-like, Paul never ran defensive drills or patterns. He didn't have to prove anything, but he was always out there working on his moves. He worked awfully hard and he had a lot of grace. Everybody had tremendous respect for the man, who was double- and triple-teamed in every game he played in. Paul Warfield wasn't the fastest guy in the world, but he had tremendous moves and was a hell of a blocker, with the ability to just flatten guys. He was the best blocker I ever saw at the position of wide receiver. He came to play every game and was a class guy who led by example. But Paul was never fond of the Shula system because they didn't throw the ball enough at that time for him.

Darryl Carlton out of Tampa was the number one pick of the Miami Dolphins in 1975. He bought a gun in a bar in Miami, and after a while decided he didn't want it. He tried to sell the gun back. They wouldn't take it back. Not the calmest guy in the world, Darryl was pissed off. He took his gun and his car and he drove—maybe he was trying to drive his troubles away. Over a bridge into another car he went. His car exploded and he almost burned himself to death. Darryl was a tackle with all sorts of problems, including very bad weight problems. He didn't last very long.

Jack Graham, a quarterback from Colorado State,

was pick number 14B for the Dolphins in the 1975 draft. He came to training camp, but he was never given a chance. They let him into the last two or three plays in practice. It was pouring down rain, and he threw a couple of skid balls, as if to prove to them that he couldn't throw a football. When the practice ended, Jack was a little down on himself.

"Do you have any other way to go?" I asked.

"Law school."

"Then go—that sounds like a good deal, a good career for you." That was basically it for him.

The first regular season NFL game that I played in was on December 1, 1975, against New England. Bob Griese had been injured the week before, and Earl Morrall hurt a knee, so I came in late in the game.

My first NFL start was December 7, 1975, against Buffalo, a team that hadn't beaten the Dolphins in eleven games. It was the first of three starts in a row, to close out the season.

People asked Bob Griese, "Do you think this guy can do the job?" And I remember what he said as if it was yesterday. "This guy can throw the football. He's very knowledgeable. All he needs is an arena."

But O. J. Simpson on Buffalo had different thoughts: "It's bad enough to lose eleven straight to a team," O. J. said. "But to think about them making it twelve in a row without either one of their two top quarterbacks— wow, that would be too much. If we can't beat Miami with Don Strock playing quarterback, we're never going to beat them."

We won the game 31–21. I completed 12 of 15 passes, including 11 in a row—short ones. That's the way the

Dolphins played football at that time—possession-type slant patterns. We didn't throw the ball down the field much. Later I thanked O. J. Simpson for giving me inspiration. It felt good. It still does.

A week later in Memorial Stadium against Baltimore, I threw a pass to Nat Moore. It was a touchdown pass but the officials said Nat was out of the end zone. If the league had instant replay then, we would have won the game. Then, with fog sweeping down, Toni Linhart of the Colts kicked a 31-yard field goal in overtime. That picture is in the Hall of Fame and still in my memory. The ball going through the fog and people jumping up and down. We lost the game, 10–7. Losses like that made 1975 the first time in six seasons with Shula as coach that the Dolphins were out of the play-offs. But in 1976, without Csonka, Warfield, and Kiick, things would get much worse.

Our number two pick in 1976 was Loaird McCreary, a tight end out of Tennessee State. Don Shula has a little bit of a lisp, and he had a heck of a time pronouncing McCreary's first name. It always came out sounding like "Lord."

That didn't suit Shula too well, so he told McCreary: "There's only one lord, so I'm going to call you 'Duke.'"

Duke was a vain kind of guy, always doing his hair in a mirror before a game; he also always made sure he color-coordinated his three sweatbands. The guy was a fusser. "I want to look good for the crowd," was his explanation. "I want the fans to take pride in seeing me out there."

Duke looked good in a uniform, but he never looked good when he was playing. The last time I saw him he was a checker behind the counter in the airport in Atlanta.

Number 4A for Miami in the 1976 draft was McCreary's teammate at Tennessee State, Melvin Mitchell. They weighed him in, and he was 29 pounds overweight. Two days later he made weight by taking water pills, Ex-Lax, and nearly starving himself to death. Melvin always had a weight problem, and that probably was the main reason he lasted only three years with Miami.

Number 10B for Miami in the draft of 1976 was Don Testerman out of Clemson, surely one of the craziest people I ever met in my life. Don was a freshman at Virginia Tech when I was a senior, but he virtually made a career out of changing schools. As I heard the story, one of the things he spent a lot of time talking about was the fun he had clowning around when he jabbed his brother several times with an ice pick. I told you we had all kinds of characters coming in with each draft.

I played sporadically in 1976, a little here, a little there. There was a lot of turmoil and a lot of problems. A couple of bright spots were wide receivers Howard Twilley, the last of the Dolphin originals, and Freddie Solomon. Howard went over the 3,000-yard mark with eight catches in an overtime loss to Kansas City. And Freddie Solomon had himself a day in a game against Buffalo—252 yards on a 79-yard punt return, a 53-yard pass play, a 59-yard flanker reverse.

But overall, the season was a horror story. It was the first losing season, the only losing season we ever had, in my years with the Dolphins. We finished the 1976 season 6–8, in third place in the Eastern Division.

Miami is a transient kind of town that always has an influx of tourists and a lot of retired people. It's always been one of the glamour franchises in the league. People always want to see the Dolphins on TV, especially if it's November or December and they're up north and it's nasty outside. There are always the palm trees and the announcer saying: "It's a beautiful day here in Miami." Instead of watching two teams slug it out in the mud and the snow, it's a pleasure for everyone to be watching Miami play in the sunshine. Through the years there's always been a great star, a marquee player on the Dolphins. And everyone has a perception of Don Shula as the great coach.

In the really great years, the early years, the Orange Bowl sold out all the time. The biggest crowds were always there when we played the New York Jets. All those New Yorkers down for vacation were always in attendance.

In 1976, we faced Joe Namath in the Orange Bowl for the last time in his career and wound up beating him and the Jets, 16–0. But even with that game and his last appearance and all, attendance was down. It kind of symbolized 1976, and the fact that everyone knew some changes were needed.

THE GAMES WITHIN THE GAME

THERE are all kinds of football games going on all the time—the one the fans see at home on TV, the one the fans see at the stadium and the game played on the field between the white lines. And there are all the wheels turning on the part of coaches, players, defense versus offense, player versus player. Once you're a part of it all, you never forget what it is like—the feel of it all, the sights, smells, sounds.

Every game is kind of the same ritual. The kickers come out fifty-five minutes before game time along with punt returners, quarterbacks, and receivers. The quarterbacks try to get warm, throw a few balls, get their touch working. They throw with the wind and against the wind, where lots of times the ball will sink on you.

Usually the kicker or backup quarterback will check the flag on top of the goalposts or on top of the tunnel to determine the swirl or drive of the wind. That was usually my job on the Dolphins. Shula would come over to me: How far this way? How far that way? How far into the wind? How far away from the wind? In that way, he'd have an idea of what could be attempted and what could not.

In the warm-up the receivers start running their routes and especially check the turf in the corners of the end zone. The kickers kick into and with the wind. The rest of the team comes out about ten minutes later to do stretching exercises and loosen up.

After all that, everybody goes back to the locker room for any kind of adjustments that are needed. That includes new pads, retaping if needed, any kind of Caine Brothers treatment if that's called for. There are always refittings of pads, strings, flaps, gloves, wraps, whatever. Some receivers and backs, in addition to using sticky gloves, wear a wrap on their legs for artificial turf. That surface doesn't give and will cut you, and it's dirty—not like your kitchen floor.

Some guys in the locker room take a sip of soda or water. Not too much of that stuff is taken, though, until players get totally into the flow of the game. Most players take advantage of the opportunity to go to the bathroom. The whole pregame ritual is a kind of cooling-down period. Coaches go over any final calls and alert guys to any special situations.

About five or six minutes before game time the whole team is assembled and the Lord's Prayer is usually said. Then an official comes into each locker room to tell the teams that there are two minutes left before they have to come out for the introductions.

Everybody knows there has been lots of preparation, and the routine is always the same game after game, but there's always that air of anticipation. I used to be thinking: Well, I know I'm prepared, but I wonder what's going to happen today. I wonder how it's going to turn out. The ball is oblong, and you can buy one of those footballs for twenty-six dollars, but there are guys today making millions killing each other for the chance to throw it, hold it in their hands, carry it, intercept it, not drop it on the ground. Everybody wants the football.

Suddenly there's the walk through the tunnel, the light, the playing field, the crowd noise, the introductions, the national anthem, and the game begins.

All the action takes place on the playing field. However, the area that is almost as crucial to how well a team does is on the sidelines where the team benches are located between both the 35-yard lines. That area, called "the 35 × 35," is part think tank, part combat zone, part rest room, part dressing room—and all football.

The area takes up 30 yards in length and there's a six-foot area in it that's painted white or yellow. Nobody is allowed in the six-foot area other than the coaches and one player. And that player on Miami was usually me, because I was sending in signals.

In the Dolphin setup the offensive line is on one side of the bench, and the defense is on the other side of the bench. There are areas where they want people to sit so if they want to talk to an offensive lineman, let's say, they know where he is.

The water and the Gatorade are right in the middle of the benches. The players who do most of the sitting on those benches are the offensive and defensive linemen. They're there sitting in between series. They do that because, as big people who undergo great exertion and wear and tear, they need to get rest whenever possible.

In the 35 × 35, there is a phone for the defense and a phone for the offense, and each goes upstairs to one of the coaches in a booth in the stands. The red phone is the quarterback phone, and it's used to communicate with the coordinator in the booth. Upstairs, there are usually four to six people.

On the field there are the head coach, the defensive coordinator, the quarterback coach or offensive coordinator, the offensive line coach, and the special teams coaches. Then there are also the equipment guys, team doctors, trainers, the team dentist, who usually has an assistant with him. Sometimes there's a priest in the 35 × 35.

In terms of numbers, including guys with oxygen and guys who work the phones, there are always about 70 people there—the 45 players and all the support for them. Sometimes there are some celebrity figures on the sidelines, but they are kept farther back.

Dan Dowe was the trainer for many years for the Dolphins, and he was succeeded by Bobby Monica, who had been his assistant. Bobby goes to the stadium in a truck hours before game time. Everything is unloaded into trucks. "Everything" includes practice gear if the team is planning to practice at the stadium, sweat pants, rain jackets, you name it. If a guy breaks his helmet, there's always another one available or the equipment to fix it right then and there. If a shoulder pad breaks, a string—immediate first aid to that stuff is available. And if it can't be done, a quick switch is made.

You always bring two or three pairs of shoes to a game. If a cleat falls out, there are extra cleats. If your shoe can't be repaired, there's always another pair to switch into. There are extra jerseys if the one you're wearing gets ripped. There are towels, sweatbands, stickum spray. Every type of weather condition is prepared for—rain, sleet, fog, snow. When the Dolphins go from warm Miami to a late-season game in a place like Cleveland, they bring along parkas, long underwear, gloves, shirts for underneath. There can be as much as 2,500 pounds of cold-weather gear for the team.

The 35 × 35 is highly organized. The tangle of wires used to be a problem, but it's a lot better now, with kids holding things together and keeping that wire straight, helping out the head coach and coordinators. It may seem messy when you watch a game in the stadium or on TV, but most of that is just from blood, sweat and tears, cleat marks, cups thrown around, and antacid pill wrappers. Everything has a place and a purpose.

It can be a dangerous area, and that's why there's a six-foot restraining line from the field to the bench area. There's six feet where no players are allowed in, because a lot of injuries have happened in that area. A couple of years ago, Neil Smith, a defensive end for Kansas City, was running after Dan Marino. He chased him out of bounds and Smith ran right into Shula and just leveled him. One time Dan Devine at Green Bay had his leg broken on a play like that. Crashes and collisions happen all the time, and in the 35 × 35 you have to be constantly aware of what is going on.

What exists in one team's 35 × 35 has to exist

equally for the other team. If you have heaters as the home team, the visiting team has to have heaters. If you have fans, the other team has to have fans. If your phones go out, the other team's phones are also shut off.

The equipment manager usually tells the nonplaying personnel what the dress code for the game will be. "This week, we will be wearing our brown shoes, our brown slacks, our brown shirts." Usually the head coaches wear a different-colored shirt.

The "Hi, Mom" has become really popular on TV now, guys clowning, mugging, making faces for the camera. Part of that is the ham in a lot of guys, but the main reason is that the camera that picks up those mug shots is stationed right behind the benches.

I recommend that the next time you attend a football game, let your eyes stray from the playing field to the 35 × 35. It's an interesting place where everything happens: play calling, decisions on personnel, on injuries. Bitching, cheering, crying, laughing, vomiting— all the good stuff that the fan rarely sees.

Another thing the fans don't see, no matter how many TV close-ups they beam at you, is what's going on in the middle of the field. In places where it's very hot, players drink as much as a gallon of liquid. There's no time for them to go back through the tunnel to relieve themselves. So guys were always urinating there— right there in the huddle. Some probably did the other thing, but I never noticed. One image that stays with me is of the modest guys, their legs crossed in the huddle in what was kind of a prevent defense.

People always ask me what it's really like playing

quarterback, being out there on the field, taking charge of a team. Well, that feeling is like nothing else in the world. For one thing I distinctly remember reaching in and getting the ball from some of those big centers. Doing that gave me the opportunity to feel more ass than I ever felt any other place. And there were several times, mostly in practice, but sometimes in a game, where those centers used to wait until I went to get the ball and then they'd pass gas. Ugh! But what could you do? I certainly wasn't going to fight them?

Yet, once the play is in action, it's strictly business out there. It's also surprising how quiet everything gets. There's a big difference between the bantering beforehand and the coming together on the line. The ball is snapped and there's a quiet, almost a hush, and then during the play, the noise starts up. It's like a lawnmower: A-A-A-H-H-H-R-R-R-AHRRRRR—and then it's over.

If you're a quarterback playing at home, and you're knocked down just as you get the pass off, and you hear the fans cheering, there's a good chance that the pass was caught or a flag was thrown for interference. But if you're at home and you're knocked down and you hear ooohs and ahhhs or boos, the ball was probably dropped or intercepted. If you're quarterbacking for the "away" team, and you throw a pass and don't see where it ends up, and there's cheering, even if you're flat on the ground, you'd better get up. That noise probably means the ball has been intercepted. But if you don't hear much of anything, that generally means that the pass was completed. The point that I'm making is that home and away situations are very different for a quarterback, and in both cases you have to train yourself to rely on your ears. That's about the only sense you have going for you.

Normally, what you do to control noise, if you're a visiting team, is you try to score as quickly as you possibly can. If you stop them, that calms the crowd down a little because they're in a frenzy from the start. If the home team goes down and scores on the first possession, you're going to have some problems. You want to put points up on your first possession to take the crowd noise out. Sometimes even using your ears is a problem on the field, especially on the road. In the huddle, the noise level can become almost deafening, so all the guys have to be disciplined enough not only to be listening to you as the quarterback, they have to be looking at you to see what you are saying. Sometimes we had to get by with just hand signals, fingers for plays. We shook helmets if we couldn't hear the audibles. We also used the silent count. But that caused a lot of miscommunication, a lot of problems.

The huddle is a phenomenon all to itself. Coming back to the huddle, we had receivers like Mark Duper and Mark Clayton, who were always chattering, saying how they could beat this guy or beat that guy. My most talkative teammate ever was Ed Newman, especially in the huddle. He had some great lines like: "Think of your family. Think of your teammates. Think of your contracts." He'd get into this deal where he'd just start talking. I remember one time we were playing Kansas City, and we had a third and eleven. We ran a sweep and gained fifteen yards. But Ed picked up a penalty for clipping or holding. So they brought us back. Now we run a play and we get the first-down yardage again. And Ed is getting into a fight with a guy. There's a shoving contest. So we have a personal foul called against us. So now we're backed up, and Ed comes walking back to the huddle, talking a blue streak.

"Ed," I snap in my quarterback's command voice, "just get your fuckin' ass in the huddle and shut up."

He goes, "You're right. I deserve to be scolded."

Ed Newman was a talker. The only thing was that a lot of times he was talking to himself.

Dwight Stephenson, who might be the best center who ever played the game, hardly ever said anything. He just went ahead and played his game. Jim Langer, Mark Dennard, and Dwight—the three Miami centers I played with—were the leaders in the huddle. They helped keep things under control.

Some guys would be making a lot of noise:

"Should we cross-block?"

"Should we trap?"

Should we do this, do that?

When any guys got too vocal or too loud, those centers took it upon themselves to quiet things down. Just a couple of lines like "Everybody shut the fuck up. Let's get to work here" would do it. And everybody would listen and get on with their business.

Banter is always there on the field in some shape or form. A lot of it is exchanged between defensive backs and wide receivers. On Cleveland, Hanford Dixon and Frank Minnifield would get into a lot of exchanges with receivers, and there was always that little nudge defensive backs give after a play is over, kind of the silent body language to let the receivers know what the score was.

There were always a lot of guys in the league who talked a good fight. Matt Millen, who played for the Raiders, was a talker. But that was after plays were over. Most guys aren't talkers during the play because they have a job or a position to handle. But after a play is over there's all that chatter or banter back and forth like: "I'm going kick your ass next play." Or "Don't try to cut me again." Or "I'll step on your face." That kind of stuff.

Between plays some defensive players relay messages to offensive players, like "Stop holding me or I'm gonna break your fucking neck," when they are walking back to huddles. A lot of guys do a lot of talking like that. And a lot of guys do a lot of talking in the papers. But very often, when you get in the heat of the battle, you don't hear a lot of talking. A team has to be ready to have it all together in a matter of seconds.

Receivers come into the huddle sometimes jabbering away: "I can beat this guy on such-and-such a pattern." Then as the quarterback you're thinking as you come to the line, after the play has been called, and you see the defense you like, you can audible to that receiver's play. A lot of the guys will tell you that they are open—they're ALWAYS open. Sometimes they're NOT!

Running backs never really say much, other than "Give me the ball." They never really tell you they're open, in terms of patterns or anything like that. And the offensive linemen are generally pretty quiet, just collecting themselves in the huddle for the job they have to do. Any talking they do is usually on the sideline: "I think we can trap this guy," or whatever.

I've always felt that the guys on the Dolphins listened. Usually, on the bench, you talked and tried to get together your thoughts about the next series on whom they could beat, and then you would try to get them lined up against those guys and go after them.

As the quarterback you're the guy who calls the play; the other guys run your play. Throughout my career in Miami, *I called all my plays*. I had control of the veterans. There was a much more businesslike situation in those early years. That was football. We threw the ball, but not a whole lot. We ran the ball a lot. It was a very physical-type team. There was a finesse to it, and there was a physical part to it. We had a lot of finesse plays: sucker traps and things like that. In the later years, we got into situation substitution. That's when we got into a problem in the huddle. On third down, you bring in two receivers, a tight end goes out, a back goes out. That's a lot of people coming in and out. So they have to be on the same frequency. And sometimes they're not.

When you're in the huddle and you call a play that you believe is going to work, your teammates sense it. You're the chessmaster, in control. If I'm calling the play, the other guys will work harder because they share the faith that I know this guy'll block and the other will get open.

I'd tell a player like Ed Newman, "We're going to run dive 34 right over your ass. We need a yard. Can we get a yard?"

"We'll get more than that."

Now the spotlight is on Ed—and don't think that sucker wasn't out there giving 110 percent. He'd blow that guy in front of him to kingdom come.

We'd gain four yards and Ed would come back to the huddle all smiles. "Thanks for calling on me."

That kind of stuff developed rapport with the guys you were playing with. But if you're out there and they send in a play that comes from the box to the coach to the field—you lose something there. Suppose you don't like the play, and you say, "This fucking play stinks!" Ten other guys hear you say that. They don't have faith that the play will work. And sometimes it doesn't work just because of no faith in it. Many times by not calling your own plays you don't get into the flow of what's going on.

On the field, one of the more interesting and goofy scenes is the pile. On a short-yardage play where you're running straight dive and you need a half yard, there's liable to be 14 or 15 of the 22 players in a stack. There are tangled bodies, and guys saying:

"Watch my fucking leg."

"Get off my balls."

It's hard work untangling, and it takes some time. The refs say, "Everybody up slowly, watch the arm, watch the leg. Okay, let him go." Because the guy who made the tackle still has a hold on the guy he picked on, the ref is kind of monitoring the whole thing, watching for leg movement and stuff like that. Unstacking the pile can make for a lot of surprises, and sometimes the ball simply winds up in the hands of the strongest or most determined guy. And the guy who originally had it goes around bitching that it was stolen or that his team was ripped off.

After a guy made a great run for a touchdown or first down on short yardage, you'd see a lineman walking through the pile trying to grab him and hug him. I've seen guys wade in and pull guys out. That was a sign of warmth and affection and was nice. But one kind of pile you always hated to see was when a receiver caught a touchdown pass close to the end zone on a big play. That's because all the linemen were running him over and trying to grab him, and they would all end up in a pile with the receiver crushed on the bottom.

Piles are just one of the weird things taking place on the field. There are plenty of others.

Back in October of 1975 we played against the Jets in New York on a rainy day. Joe Namath was basically all they had at the time, and he thought if the hole was round enough he'd be able to throw the ball through it. We intercepted him six times and beat the Jets, 45–0. But the thing that stands out in my mind from that game, strangely enough, is a guy named Johnny Jones—the backup quarterback who came in for Joe Willie.

Our No-Name Defense ran Jones off the field right in front of our bench, and when he came close it was clear that under his helmet he was wearing a rain hood. That sure attracted Don Shula's attention. "Look at that guy. Look at what the hell he is wearing. How bad does he want to play this game?"

A guy who wanted to play the game with all he had was one of my favorite teammates, Larry Seiple. One game he was running a pattern and he took a tremendous shot. He came out of there and was lying on the sideline, pushing his legs back and forth.

"What the hell happened to you?" I asked.

He goes, "I got kicked in the balls."

I say, "Yeah, right."

The next day we came in for a little treatment, and his balls were all shriveled up, just black and blue. It had to be so painful.

"I guess," I told him, "we're going to have to put you on injured reserve, with broken balls or something."

I threw a touchdown pass to Duriel Harris against the Eagles in the Orange Bowl on a Monday Night. Making that catch excited him so that he jumped up and tried to spike the ball over the goalpost and twisted his knee and was out for a couple of weeks. I still have a laugh about that.

Marv Fleming is a California guy, very soft-spoken. He played the right position—tight end. Man, he was tight with a dollar. The *Miami News* at that time sold for a dime, and I borrowed the ten cents from him one day.

The next day I saw him and gave him a dime. He goes, "No, Jack," he called everybody "Jack." "It's eleven cents."

"Eleven cents?"

"You know, interest." So I gave him eleven cents.

Around that time Marv caught a touchdown pass in the end zone in Buffalo. When he came down with the ball, he happened to land on a ten-dollar bill that was lying there in the end zone. Usually, Marv didn't show that much emotion. But this time he was lit up and smiling as he came off the field. It looked to me like he was happier over finding the ten-dollar bill than he was that he scored the TD.

Between the lines there are all kind of tricks of the trade, and I think that quarterbacks know most of them. We used to bob our head to draw defensive offsides. That worked like a charm for a while. Then the officials started catching on and giving out warnings that there would be penalties for doing that. So we went to moving our head side-to-side, where you're not really bobbing. That worked for a while, until they started calling that, too. Then I went to moving my knees just a little bit. The defensive line is taught to move on the movement of the ball. But when they see any quiver, like knee movement, it's like a gong is setting them off. I got a lot of offsides in that maneuver. Many other quarterbacks have done the same thing with the same results.

Fred Smerlas was an easy target. Whenever we played Buffalo, the quarterbacks always made a mental note: "Vary cadence...and anytime you want him, you've got him." That's what I did with Smerlas and with others—changed the cadence and got the offsides penalty.

Knowing how to get time-outs when you wanted them was another part of the inner game. I would tell the ref: "OK, we're just going to run this play and then I want a TO right away." The official knows you have to signal for the time-out, but if you make him aware that you're going for it, you get him to look at you and look for it. A little nuance like that might, at times, wind up being the difference between winning and losing a game. The game is one of inches and seconds. Just getting an extra second or two by alerting the official is a key maneuver.

The thing that John Madden said is so true: if an official marks the ball with his left foot, most of the time it's a first down. If he marks it with his right foot, chances are it's going to be just a hair short. Whether the ball's right in the middle of his foot also makes a difference. Guys are always arguing about where they spot the ball.

"Fuck you, it was here!"

"The ball was here!"

"They pushed him back!"

"No, the ball was here."

They're always lobbying. But once the official sets his foot, that's it. They're not going to change it.

I once threw a pass to the left side in a preseason game. The receiver caught the ball, and got hit simultaneously—his feet were in. But they ran him right into the referee and knocked him down, too. The ref was looking around for help, and nobody else knew what was going on. It was obvious that the receiver was in, but the ref got knocked down and he couldn't make the call. So the decision was made to replay the down. That's the only time I've ever been in a game where that happened. I said to another ref: "We can't replay the down, you know he was in. You saw it was in!"

"It was his call, Don, and I can't call it from back here. It was close."

"You KNOW he was in."

"Well, we're going to replay the down." Now Shula's going crazy on the sideline.

So I said, "I'll tell you what. You go over and tell that

man over there that we're replaying the down. 'Cause I'm not."

Shula's going, "What the hell's going on? What's going on out there?"

So this ref goes over and tells him, and Shula says, "I've never heard of replaying a down before."

We replayed it. Talk about instant replay.

Coaches and refs—now that's a whole another area. All coaches work refs in a way. They all know them personally.

Before games, we'd look at a program to see who was working a game, who was the head guy. Some guys take care of quarterbacks, refs like Jim Tunney, Gene Barth, Fred Wyatt.

Defensive linebackers are allowed no more than two steps after the whistle blows before they hit the quarterback. This ref might give a step and a half; another one might give three. There were guys who were a little more lenient for defensive linemen, so you always checked to see who was there. You also knew who was lenient and who was not, among the officials—in terms of the out of bounds, in terms of possessions and catches. And you might set up plays there accordingly.

Some officials also ran a very fast clock. (Today with a 45-second clock, there's no longer such a thing as a fast- or a slow-clock official.) But when we had only 30 seconds to play with, we referred to an offensive and defensive clock. One guy might wait till the ball was spotted and signal; another guy might wait until the moment the receivers were back. You had to remember the clock rate of officials, and if you did, a lot of time you could make that knowledge work for you.

I was one of the first players in the NFL to stay in that six-foot area on the sidelines—the one player along with the coaches. Everybody was always yelling, "Get behind the line, get behind the line." And I would say to the ref: "Jack, you know, I'm allowed in here."

"Okay, Don, you are allowed there."

"Thanks, Jack," I'd say. "I appreciate it." Then I would talk to the official all during the game, keeping up a kind of running patter.

"You know that strong safety...?"

"Yeah, I'm familiar with him."

"Well, he's not that good a cover guy."

"He doesn't look too bad."

"Well, he's been holding our tight end the last two or three plays. He can't cover a damn. We got that in our scouting report."

That was the way I said it, not like, "Watch this asshole!" The gamesmanship usually worked.

The answer I'd get was, "Okay, Don, we'll keep an eye on him."

Maybe ten plays later we would have a pass play coming up and the official would be in earshot. "We've got a pass," I'd say. "I hope that guy doesn't hold this time, too."

Then as soon as there was any kind of contact, the flag was thrown and the call was made for holding. Sometimes there was interference and sometimes there was a hit, but what I did was put that circumstance in the mind of the official. The power of influence. That was just one of the little nuances of the games.

One of the Dolphin special tricks of the trade involved silicone. Assistant head coach John Sandusky's first wife Ruth was a highly skilled seamstress. Players on our offensive line would go to her house for a fitting. She'd make their shirts so form-fitting they were like an outer skin. Before games our offensive line would go into the shower room fully dressed, and silicone would be sprayed all over their jerseys. It was a little edge, but it was an edge. Opposing players were never able to grab hold of or tear off the jerseys of our offensive line players.

Stickum is another tool of the trade. Fred Biletnikoff used to have it on his socks, on his wristbands. He could catch the ball with one hand, he had so much stuff. Lester Hayes did the same thing. Stickum is banned in the National Football League today. But stickum is all over the place. Guys use stickum sprays on the sidelines and put that stuff on their hands and all over their body. On the field they get the stickum off towels or belts.

As you know, a lot of games are played in the coldest of weather conditions, and tools of the trade exist to try to help out in those situations, too. You probably have noticed the little pouch some players have just over their belly button. No, I don't mean the type sported by William "the Fridge" Perry. I'm talking about the one made out of cloth. In that pouch is a little shake-bag. If you shook the bag up, it got hot, and was just the thing for keeping your hands warm. In Cleveland, we had these pouches in the front with fur in them. That worked well, too just like having a fur-lined coat. Also in Cleveland, there was something to keep your feet warm. They called it atomic balm. It was red-hot stuff that players would rub on their feet. Then they would tape up little plastic bags around their feet to keep the warmth of the atomic balm in. Pantyhose, too, are used for warmth. It was hysterical to watch these guys put them on. I remember Larry Little was fond of putting on "Big Momma" pantyhose. He would ruin three or four pair just popping holes in them while he struggled to put them on.

There's not much that has been invented as far as tricks of the trade concerning the pigskin. What you see is what you get—most times. There are twenty-four footballs available at all times. You can't just change a football when you want to. The officials control that. The only hanky-panky I ever noticed as far as footballs are concerned is how many times I saw the ball come out drier for the home team than for the visiting team.

The wet ball is the curse of the quarterback; and in the pros, aside from wiping and wiping, there's not much you can do about it. But when I was in college, we had a wet-ball trick. We'd take thumbtacks, and our trainer would file them all the way to nubs. He'd take those nubs and tape them with skin-colored tape to all your fingers except your thumb. And then we'd go into a gym before the game, if it was raining outside, and dip balls into buckets of water. We'd spend some time practicing throwing those balls.

An assistant coach told me one time: "Listen, if the referee comes up to you before a game, just walk away from him and wait for me to come down from the box. Just put your hand behind your back and walk away." But the problem with the thumbtack trick is that when a ball gets wet, it gets little marks in it from these tacks. You'd get little rip marks in the ball from where your fingers were when you let go. I said, "What's going to happen if they see the marks?"

"Well, don't worry about it. They change balls so often, you might be able to get through a whole game without anyone really knowing what's going on."

We never actually used the trick in a game, but we were prepared to do it. Our trainer had a file full of these thumbtacks. I always wondered what it might have been like.

The football itself, being oblong and taking all those crazy rolls and bounces, is a subject that a whole chapter or even a book could be devoted to. There are tricks to running it, catching it, kicking it, holding it. There are a lot of interesting nuances about the relationship between the quarterback and the football.

Throwing the football is not an arm thing. It's not like the old college "Street and Smith" shit—the quarterback posed with the ball behind his ear. Everybody throws the ball differently. Some guys throw it with the point up to the receiver—that makes it easier to catch. Bob Griese threw it that way. But Dan Marino's motion makes the ball come to the receiver with the point down, and coming in that way it may be a little tougher to catch. Terry Bradshaw and Johnny Unitas put their index finger at the back point of the ball to get rotation. Fran Tarkenton held the ball in the middle with his hand all over the seams. Bradshaw threw very few spirals, but Kenny Stabler, game in and game out, threw perfect spirals. They both got results, so being effective doesn't mean that you have to throw spirals all the time.

But all of that is nuance. It's the basic principles that have to be operating for a quarterback to be successful. The whole trick to throwing the ball is to bring your arm back and then use your hips to bring your arm forward. The actual motion of bringing your hand forward gets your hand reversed, and that twists your wrist. It's like you're throwing a screwball in baseball. Then the perfect follow-through takes place when you whip your hips, winding up with your hand hitting right between your legs and with your belt buckle facing your target. No matter what position your body is twisted in, if you face your belt buckle to your receiver you'll get the ball to him. The belt buckle is key.

Dan Henning, my old college coach who now is head man with San Diego, told me: "Out of a thousand passes, you'll be able to set up perfectly maybe fifty times." So realizing this, I knew how important it was to have that old belt buckle pointed in the right direction to get the ball to the target.

Stride is another important thing in throwing the ball. "When you throw, remember," Henning told me, "even a man six six can turn himself into five nine by taking too long a stride, forcing a high pass or overthrow." I always remembered that and worked on the right stride, nice and natural. Today when you watch a game and the ball comes in too hard or floats out there like a duck, a lot of the problem comes from overstriding or no striding on the part of the quarterback.

A move that I always used that involves seven steps

back and two steps shuffling forward is a basic maneuver for most quarterbacks. It's what they mean when they say, "He's stepping up into the pocket." It helps prevent the sack by allowing you to keep your friends around you sort of like an umbrella. Marino and Montana do it all the time—the steps and the slide—and are adept at it. But I am amazed that lots of other quarterbacks don't use that move. And they sometimes pay the price for not using it.

Another part of the quarterback's bag of tricks is trying always to look for mismatches or any other edge. If the opposition has a defensive back who can't cover your receiver deep, you exploit that. If you have a player who has trouble adjusting in the bump-and-run, you compensate. If you have a guy on your team who has trouble running the deep comeback, you change your formation to get your player to run that maneuver against someone he can do well against. Personnel on both sides dictate what goes on. Mark Gastineau on the Jets was a force, but he was never great against the run, so we ran draws inside of him to get that edge in the battle.

Against the Pittsburgh Steelers in their great years, adjustment was almost impossible. They had the best of the best defensive units ever put together. How'd you like to have to line up and play against these guys?

Across the line was Mean Joe Greene, Dwight White, L. C. Greenwood, Steve Furness. The linebackers were Jack Ham, Jack Lambert, Andy Russell—probably three of the best that ever played together. They had Donnie Shell at strong safety and Mike Wagner at weak safety, Mel Blount at one corner and Dwayne Woodruff or J. T.

Thomas at the other. It was tough going against them, even a little scary. The defensive coordinator was Bud Carson, released in 1990 as head coach of the Cleveland Browns. Maybe he wasn't cut out to be a head coach, but he was a hell of a defensive coordinator.

About the only thing you could do against that Steel Curtain defense of Pittsburgh as a running play was to go to the left side away from L. C. and Mean Joe Greene. But that wasn't doing too much.

Minnesota, with the Marshalls, Pages, Ellers, was a terrific pass rushing team with great linebackers. About the only tactic against them was to just try to slow them down. The old LA Rams with Jack Youngblood and Fred Dryer and Merlin Olsen at defensive tackle also killed offenses. Cutting the legs out from under their pass rush was one tactic that sometimes worked.

Against players like Andre Tippet, a big strong martial arts type, or Lawrence Taylor, we on Miami knew it was no contest having a running back out there to block them. So we'd slide out an offensive lineman or tackle to block. That was easy in the Miami scheme with the centers we had like Dwight Stephenson, Jim Langer.

The joke for a while was that our offensive linemen were nothing but "mushrooms." That's what Bob Kuechenberg and Jim Langer used to call themselves. "Nobody tells us about the passing game or about any special plays," they would gripe. "We're like mushrooms," they'd say. "All they do is feed us shit and let us sit in the dark."

But that kind of talk is just a put-on. The game of modern football demands intelligence. They were intelligent guys. There aren't many around playing the game who aren't intelligent in a football way.

Intelligence among football players is misunderstood and misinterpreted. And so are statistics.

What does the completion percentage mean? You see a guy completes 62.5 percent. Another guy has a percentage of 67.8. Those stats mean absolutely nothing, especially if a team loses a game by 14 points. A lot of quarterbacks have won the Super Bowl in recent years, and aside from Joe Montana, their completion percentage was not that high, but their yards per attempt was.

Jim Plunkett is a perfect example of what I'm talking about. He only completed about 50 percent of his passes, but when he connected he was able to complete a first-down most of the time.

Today I see guys jacking up their stats throwing two-yard completions. They'll throw the ball on third and eight and hope their receiver breaks the tackle and gets the first down or more.

The big deal now is third-down completion percentage. The 1989 Dolphins were 8–8 and led the league in pass completion percentage on third down. All that meant was that on first and second down they weren't doing much. It's like the old line: figures lie and liars figure.

Another part of the game within the game is instant replay. In 1990, they barely made the vote to retain instant replay. It passed by one vote, and that's only because they put a two-minute time limit on making a decision. And, again in 1991 it barely squeaked by when the owners voted. But I still believe its days are numbered.

It's sick to think that the fate of coaches, teams, that play-off chances, rest with the decisions being made by some retired officials looking at pictures under the pressure of a two-minute deadline.

Before, the people up in the booth could take twenty minutes until they came up with the final verdict. They never took all that time, but there were cases where they took ten or twelve minutes to decide. A score could have been 27–7 with three minutes left in a game, and they'd go and buzz down to replay some bit of nonsense. That was what pushed the league into going for the two-minute limit. That and the fact that it's a game for commercials.

Two minutes mean nothing. In some games eight cameras are used. In others there are four; in others there are twelve. But the number of cameras has nothing to do with perspective.

I am opposed to instant replay. The NFL existed for decades before they brought that damn thing in. Instant replay has no place in the game. Professional football is an action game, a physical game. But all the momentum is broken with instant replay to see if a guy's foot is in or out of bounds. They don't have instant replay for holding calls or tripping calls. If the ball is kicked high over the goalposts, one guy says whether it's good or not—they don't replay those kicks. The whole policy is inconsistent. And what about all those games played before instant replay came into the NFL? Should there be an asterisk in the record book to show games decided by instant replay?

With instant replay, everybody waits. The officials don't miss many. There are very few plays that are reviewed that are overturned. That should tell you something. So should hearing over and over again: "The play stands as ruled, first down...."

No team, no coach, no players can get a replay to take place. They'll all yell about it but not till the guy in the box buzzes the official on the field is there a chance for a review. It's like a leash from upstairs in the box attached to an official who is right there amidst the action.

The wrong decision can cost a team a chance to get into the play-offs or the Super Bowl. When I was in Cleveland in 1988, we were playing against Houston, and Warren Moon threw a lateral that Clay Mathews recovered for Cleveland. He picked the ball up and went into the end zone. The instant replay ruling was that the ball was dead at the spot of the recovery, that it was a lateral and it's Houston's ball. I didn't follow it. But instant replay cost Cleveland a chance to go on to another game to play Buffalo in Buffalo.

On two straight Mondays in October of 1990 the ridiculousness of instant replay was there for all to see. In a game between Philadelphia and Minnesota, Calvin Williams, the wide receiver on the Eagles, was awarded a touchdown in the first period. He had one foot out of bounds. ABC's Al Michaels made a big deal out of pointing out that as soon as instant replay springs into action the play would be overturned. But wouldn't you know? The play stood because they decided Carl Lee of Minnesota had pushed Williams out of bounds just as he was catching the ball. It didn't look like Lee did any pushing, but the play was not up for review since it was a judgment call by the official. That was for starters. In the second period there was a replay that showed that Herschel Walker of the Vikings fumbled the ball and that it should have gone over to Philadelphia. It didn't. They couldn't overturn the play because the whistle was blown early.

The next week in the game between the Bengals and the Browns, three minutes were wasted before the replay official came to the decision that Bernie Kosar had made a lateral and not a forward pass on a first-down play. But possession was retained by the Browns anyway. Talk about crazy, though. The officials somehow lost track of the downs during the delay for the instant replay. Bernie threw an incompletion on the next play, and the marker on the sideline indicated that Cleveland was now on fourth down. That led to a steambath of indecision—five minutes worth before the officials finally realized it was third down.

Sure the camera is better than the human eye, but only if there's enough time to review all the camera can show you. And you can't see much under two minutes of pressure. Instant replay is a toy, a gimmick, especially as it's now used. I say get rid of it and let the guys play the game the way it's supposed to be played, free of interruptions that do more harm than good.

THE
MIDDLE YEARS:
1977–1982

IN 1977, the number one and number two picks of the Miami Dolphins were A. J. Duhe and Bob Baumhower. Shula was elated that he got those two talented players. He was enjoying his dinner that night. Then he got the word that two of our stars, Don Reese and Randy Crowder, were busted for trying to sell a pound of cocaine to undercover police officers.

Up and down. That's football. That's life. Duhe and Baumhower were on the spot. Those guys had to become instant starters, and they did.

In May of 1977 Earl Morrall retired. He was 43 years old and had thrown for 20,809 yards in his 21-year career. Only Bob Griese and myself were there, so quarterback Steve Spurrier, who was released by Tampa Bay, was brought into camp. He was there for a week or so, and then he was gone. I was told that the quarterback job was wide open, which I knew was suspect.

The main quarterback job belonged to Bob Griese, and he deserved it. His "thinking man's quarterback" image became even more pronounced when he gave up the contact lenses that gave him some problems and switched to wearing regular eyeglasses. I played very sparingly in 1977. The only action I saw was Thanksgiving Day against the Cardinals in St. Louis. Our offensive attack gained 503 yards, and Bob Griese threw six touchdown passes. We ended up beating them 55–14, stopping their six-game win streak.

When Bob was inducted into the Pro Football Hall of Fame, Don Shula reminisced about that game and said he asked Bob whether he wanted to stay in. What actually happened was I told Bob: "Stay in and try to get a record seventh touchdown pass." I wouldn't go in until he tried.

Bob actually threw his seventh, but Loaird McCreary dropped the ball in the corner of the end zone. That's when Bob came out of the game.

So a lot of people have different memories of that game, but what is remembered most of all is the big brawl that took place after Conrad Dobler took a "cheap" shot at our defensive end, Vern Den Herder, and blew out his knee. It was not a pretty scene. Guys started pounding away at each other, tackling, kicking. For the Dolphins, it was like a policing action, a show on our part that there would be no "cheap" shots tolerated.

It took the officials quite a while to get guys separated, and there was a lot of cursing even after the bodies were pulled apart. I watched the whole thing from the sidelines along with the other quarterbacks. That kind of stuff was not for us—there were too many angry, big people out there.

A Miami reporter had written that the Dolphins would be the turkeys that Thanksgiving Day. That upset some of our guys. When the game ended, the reporter was in the locker room poking around, and one of our players grabbed hold of him and threw him into the shower.

"Apologize," he was yelling at him. "Apologize to the whole fucking team for that shit you wrote." It was ugly. I stayed away from the big fight on the field, but this time I got involved helping to pull that angry teammate of mine off the reporter. He could have gotten hurt pretty bad.

Conrad Dobler not only was thrown out of the game, but was also suspended, and that added some more to his media image as a tough guy, a dirty player. Dobler did do some questionable things during his career. But the media added to it, reporting that he spit in guys' faces, that he bit other players in the pile. He never did any of that to players on our team.

I can't honestly say that Dobler or any other players have been out there trying to maim or injure others. Pro football is a career for everyone, and no one wants to end someone's career. Of course, there are always the cheap shots and late shots. But I don't know how intentional those have been. No one goes out there planning to hit a guy late.

A lot was made of Jack Tatum breaking Daryl Stingley's neck and leaving him paralyzed. That was very sad, but Tatum was not out there intentionally trying to maim Stingley. They had a head-on collision in the heat of the game.

You always heard about the bad Raiders. They were physical. Howie Long bragged: "I'm an artist, only my art is to assault people." But as I saw it, Howie Long never took a cheap shot.

John Matuszak of the Raiders said: "I don't concentrate on intimidating them as much as I concentrate on kicking their ass." He did kick ass, but John, too, was not a cheap-shot artist.

Lyle Alzado might have ripped somebody's helmet off in a discussion, but I don't consider him to have been a dirty player. Lester Hayes would irritate and aggravate receivers. That made him aggressive, but he was not dirty. Lester was just out there looking to win the battle any way he could and get the mental edge.

I played against the Steelers, who were as physical as you get back in their glory years with the Steel Curtain. Everyone talked abut Mean Joe Greene. But he wasn't mean in a dirty way. Jack Lambert on the Steelers hit as hard as anyone, but he did it within the rules of the game, never tried to maim anybody. Jake Scott on the Dolphins played with a kind of wild abandon, throwing his body at people. That was his style, but he was not out there trying to hurt somebody. All of those guys are in the spirit of what Steve Owen, the New York Giants coach in the 1940s, said, "Football was invented by a mean son of a bitch—and that's the way the game's supposed to be played.

Nowadays there's all the talk about "bounties" and "bounty hunters," and a lot of it is just plain gossip. In 1990, it was rumored and reported in the Miami paper that Jim Jensen was going around talking about a $100 bounty that was supposed to have been placed on him by Philadelphia coach Buddy Ryan. That came after Miami beat the Eagles in a game in week 14. According to Jensen, players on the Eagles told Dolphin defensive end Jeff Cross that a bounty was there for the taking for the Philly player who made the best hit on Jim. Later the whole thing was made light of by Jensen when he said: "If there was a bounty, then I am disappointed that it was only $100. I'm worth more than that."

Cheap shots, bounties, takedowns, what have you—there have always been the headlines and the controversy over violence in the game of pro football. But I maintain the violence you all see is not premeditated.

What happens is that players are out there, especially late in a game, and the adrenaline is flowing hot, and it's hard to hear a whistle. Guys want to win. They go all out, and sometimes there is a violent moment. But that's not to say they're out there intentionally wanting to maim another human being.

A dirty player, someone who game in and game out takes cheap shots, could not survive in the National Football League. I'm not even talking about payback by other players. A guy who is dirty game after game would be cleaned out by his own coach, who would not tolerate that kind of behavior. I know for a fact that cheap-shot artists would have a very difficult time playing for the coaches I played for: Don Shula, Ron Meyer, and Marty Shottenheimer. They just wouldn't put up with them.

The fighting in that 1977 Thanksgiving Day game against the Cardinals got a lot of headlines, but it was just another one of Bob Griese's fabulous games in 1977. He was just superb game after game that season and was picked by the Maxwell Club of Philadelphia as its Pro Player of the Year.

I threw hundreds of balls in practice that year and sent in hundreds of hand signals to Bob. But I threw just four passes in games that whole season. That was perfectly understandable: no quarterback in the league had the numbers and quality playing time Bob Griese put out.

In 1978, with only me on the scene to back up Griese, Bill Kenney, a quarterback out of Northern Colorado, was picked 12B. He was very green. One day we had a passing drill, and Bill Arnsparger was standing in the middle of the field watching the action. The backs were running patterns against linebackers. Kenney fired the ball, and it hit Arnsparger hard, right in the middle of the ear. Down like a shot, blood trickling from his ear, Arnsparger seemed to have been in serious trouble. But he was all right once he stood up. The same couldn't be said about Bill Kenney, who had his last day of practice with the Miami Dolphins, but went on to play for a long time with the Kansas City Chiefs.

In August of 1978 against Tampa Bay in the very last preseason game, Bob Griese suffered torn ligaments in his left knee. I was pressed into service as the starting quarterback. I completed 65 of 125 passes and led the Dolphins to a 5–2 record and we were tied for first place when Bob came back. I received a lot of good press and started to think a little bit about what it would be like to be a number one quarterback somewhere. But that was just wishful thinking.

The game that stands out the most for me in that stretch of seven was played in Philadelphia. It was sort of a homecoming for me, being back in my old stomping grounds in Pennsylvania. I bought 97 tickets for the game—for all the friends and relatives who showed up. I was only paid back for about 28, so a lot of people still owe me money. I wonder how I'll collect?

In 1979, Glenn Blackwood, a safety from the University of Texas, became a Dolphin as the team's 8B selection in the draft. Miami got his pick from Denver for the rights to Jim Kiick. Carl Taseff had gone to Texas to scout one guy and ended up looking at another who kept making tackles. That was Glenn Blackwood. Shula took a chance. In 1981–82, Glenn's brother Lyle was released by the Colts and picked up by the Dolphins. They were one of the few brother acts I ever played with.

Tony Nathan out of Alabama was picked number 3A in the draft by Miami in 1979. He was a pick the Dolphins got for trading Randy Crowder to Tampa Bay. Tony Nathan is the kind of player you pencil into the lineup and forget about. It's like an Ozzie Smith in baseball, shortstop forever, or Larry Bird in basketball, forward forever. Tony was there at running back for Miami for about ten years. You could count on him. Year in, year out, day in, day out, he worked with the new guys coming in, teaching them how to play his position.

Larry Csonka was 32 years old—an old face but a new presence—when he returned to the Dolphins in 1979. This was after his three-year stint with the New York Giants, where he had gone when the World

Football League ended. We used him up the same way—like a battering ram.

In 1979, Uwe von Schamann from Oklahoma was Miami's number 7 pick in the draft. I was the holder for field-goal kickers. I had held for Garo Yepremian who was a left-footed kicker, and Uwe was right-footed. The decision was going to be made as to whose job was on the line. It was a pressure time for Garo and Uwe, but not the easiest for me either. It doesn't get much tougher than that for any professional athlete. All I had to do was tilt the ball one way or the other—the wrong way—and the kick probably wouldn't be made. I had to explain to both guys that I wouldn't screw them.

Uwe was a rookie, and Garo was a guy who had become a good friend, a guy I had held for when he tied the record for most field goals in row. But to me they were both equal—just two guys out there showing off their stuff. The coaching staff observed, measured, talked, graded both men. And the choice was Uwe. It seemed the consensus was that he had the stronger leg.

There's very little talk between the holder and the kicker. When they come in, they know what they have to do. You pick a spot out, look at him. The kicker says, "OK" or "Ready." You say, "Ready, set . . ." You take the snap. He kicks the ball.

The first kick, and probably the worst kick, of Uwe's professional career was at Rich Stadium in Buffalo. I held, and he kicked the ball low. It was blocked and a defensive back picked it up and started running. No one else knew what was going on. So I was the only one to chase him. He went 80 yards for a touchdown. Talk about being winded.

Our final game of 1979 was against the Jets. We had already clinched the division, and Shula gave me the start. There were actually four quarterbacks on the Dolphin roster that year—and that's a good trivia question for those of you who think you really know football. Bob Griese, me, Guy Benjamin out of Stanford, who was a rookie, and Bruce Hardy. Bruce had been a tight end at Arizona State, but also could play quarterback. At one time he was *Sports Illustrated* athlete of the year in America. A solid player, a smart guy, Bruce was my roommate for nine years.

I had a pretty good game against the Jets, throwing for 322 yards. Late in the game we had a chance to win or play for a tie. On the sidelines Shula said he wanted the win. So on fourth down we went for it, and Mark Gastineau and Joe Klecko and the rest of those rough tough guys on the Jets went for me. Gastineau had a kind of negative image, but he wasn't a real bad guy. He did the sack dance and all that, but it was more self-promotional stuff for the press than anything else.

Gastineau and Klecko flushed me out of the pocket. I tried to fumble the ball out of bounds but I couldn't make it. There was a wild scramble and the Jets recovered the ball. They wound up beating us 27–24. That was a typical Jet-Dolphin battle.

Some of the greatest and most competitive games were played between the Jets and the Dolphins. There were always the battles on the field and also in the stands. Some of the best fights I've ever seen took place in the stands; we used to turn around and watch guys standing toe to toe slugging it out. Man, they got more physical sometimes in the stands than we did on the field. Verbally, the games between the Dolphins and the Jets seemed to always be an exercise in who could scream louder and dirtier.

Don Shula and Jet coach Walt Michaels never got along very well—and that's an understatement. I'm not too sure that Joe Walton, when he coached the Jets, was very big on Shula's list either.

In Miami, there was this bugaboo about the Jets because they always seemed to be able to have the ability to beat us at any time no matter how lousy they were in the standings. Some teams match up well against other teams. Their receivers seemed to match up well against our defensive backs, especially a guy like Al Toon against one of our smaller backs. Their tight ends, Mickey Shuler and Rocky Cleaver, seemed to do well against our linebackers, who weren't especially great cover guys. The Jets always had that little edge, and Ken O'Brien managed some of his best quarterbacking days against us.

After we finished the 1979 season, winning the Eastern Division title, we went up to Steeltown to play in the opening game of the play-offs. Pittsburgh hammered us real good, 34–14. I came in at the end of that game, a game that was to be Larry Csonka's last one as a professional. After that season, Larry got into a contract hassle with management. He held out, wanting as much money as Delvin Williams, the running back from Kansas. It got pretty ugly. Management spread to the newspapers all the dirty laundry about what Csonka was asking for. Larry wouldn't sign, and he quit. He never played another down in professional football. As for Delvin, he was out of the league before the 1980 season ended.

The 1980 draft brought one of my all-time favorite players to the Dolphins—Joe Rose, number 7, tight end out of California. Joe "Kokomo" Rose shaved patches on his face sometimes during training camp and combed his hair straight forward to look like a dunce. He did all of those things to liven guys up. A great prankster, Joe is the kind of guy every team needs.

The 1980 draft also saw David Woodley, the 8B pick, a quarterback out of Louisiana State, come to the Dolphins. That was when everyone was running the option, and quarterbacks were running all over the place. Shula thought this guy was the answer. Woodley was a by-himself type of person, smart but not a football-instinct guy. I dealt with him as a teammate, but we didn't have a whole lot in common. I tried to give him tips into tricks of the trade, but he wasn't too interested.

That was the start of what they called the "Wood-Strock" era. Griese was still there, but on October 5, 1980, he tore his shoulder up. No one knew it when it happened, but that was to be the last game he ever suited up for and played in. Injuries took their toll on Bob—the tough hits through the years, a broken leg, various torn muscles.

For fifteen years with the Dolphins I always called my own plays; so did Bob Griese and Earl Morrall. We didn't have any plays called by the coaches until David Woodley came onto the scene. I guess Don Shula liked the idea of doing it so much that he kept on doing it.

But I wound up calling a lot of plays for Shula. He'll deny that I did, but just ask my teammates—they'll tell you that was what went on.

We began 1980 playing up in Buffalo, and they beat us for the first time in twenty tries in ten years. I saw some action near the end of the game and was down near their twenty-yard line when the clock ran out. I tried to sprint off the field and had no chance. The people there were like animals released from a cage. They were going berserk, like they had won the Super Bowl. They tore down the goalposts and were having a picnic on the field. Police were all over the place. I had to literally fight my way through the crowd to get back into the tunnel. The whole scene was kind of a metaphor for the Wood-Strock years.

Woodley was given most of the starts after Griese was hurt. But I played in most of the games that were crucial for us. The press called it the era of the two-headed quarterback. It was uncomfortable for me because I never knew when I was going to be inserted into a game. The plays were called on the sidelines by myself and Coach Shula. If things didn't work out, Shula would put me in the game. He did it many times and in many different situations, whether we were winning or losing. It was a very tough position to be in.

In 1981, the number 11 Dolphin draft pick was Jim Jensen. He had played quarterback at Boston University, where he ran the option and pitched to the tailback and blocked for him. But there was no chance for him to do that kind of stuff with Miami. Jim's tools were only there in terms of necessity.

"Just tell them you want to play on special teams," I told him. "That'll get you a chance to stick with the team." He did, and they liked what they saw. And Jim's been there ever since, better every year. I nicknamed him "Crash." Here's a guy who has played backup holder for kickers, played quarterback, tight end, both wide receivers, both running backs, and all special teams. Our number one draft pick in 1981, David Overstreet out of Oklahoma, never worked out. He went to the Canadian Football League. Later he came back to the Dolphins and died in a car crash. Another of the tragedies.

Being a realist and realizing I was in a no-win situation during the Wood-Strock years, I just kept myself sharp and ready to do anything I could for the team. Any quarterback needs a concentrated period of time to play well, to get his momentum and rhythm going. But it never worked out that way for me. I was playing a quarter of a game here, a half a game there. Whenever I played, it was always like there was someone looking over my shoulder. That time was not a high point in my career. When I was in there and things weren't going that well for me or the team, Shula didn't hesitate to make a change. That was another tough position for me to be in.

I guess the seesaw way "Wood-Strock" worked was really there for all to see on January 2, 1982. It was a contest the Pro Football Hall of Fame voted "The NFL's Greatest Game of the 1980s"—San Diego versus Miami. Eleven team records were set in the fourth longest game in NFL history, including most points (79) and most total yards (1,036). It took place beginning in late-afternoon sunshine and ending in darkness, taking four hours and three minutes of playing time. It was the first game in NFL history in which two quarterbacks passed for more than 400 yards. It was the wildest, highest-scoring football game, the most exciting game in National Football League history. And I'll never forget being out there, being a part of it all.

Clemson and Nebraska had played the night before in the Orange Bowl. Now it was our turn. The temperature was in the high 70s, but the humidity was very high. We all knew there would be a lot of sweating out there and lots of tired football players when the game came to its conclusion.

The way the game started, some guys had the feeling that it should have never begun. Three plays away from the end of the first quarter, we had no yards at all. San Diego had a 97–0 yardage spread over us. We were just throwing the game away to the most dominant offensive force in football. The booing started in the opening minutes and kept getting louder.

With 12:05 to play in the second quarter, the crowd of 73,735 in the Orange Bowl was getting more and more hostile to the Dolphins. We were down 24–0, but we had outright given them those 24 points. We didn't field a kickoff. They returned a punt. They intercepted a pass. They led 24–0 even though they only had one drive of more than 20 yards. And there I was coming in to replace David Woodley at quarterback. Talk about being fed to the slaughter!

We got three points when Uwe von Schamann kicked

a field goal. We got seven more when I threw a touchdown pass to Joe Rose.

We took a time-out with just a few seconds left in the second quarter. Don Shula said: "How about 87 circle curl lateral?"

"Sounds good to me."

"Which side?"

"Let's do it on the right side. The defender there is more aggressive."

I went back onto the field. The play we set up was the fleaflicker.

I threw a 15-yard pass to wide receiver Duriel Harris who lateraled to Tony Nathan who ran 25 yards for a touchdown, and the clock ran out. The first thing I looked for were flags, and when I didn't see any, I knew we were back in the game. That fleaflicker set off one of the most deafening roars I have ever heard in a football stadium. And the noise kept up. The people there were so charged up they even were booing the half-time show. They couldn't wait for us to come out onto the field so the game could continue. What was amazing about that fleaflicker play was that every junior high-school team has it. But it worked in a professional game. When that thing worked, it gave us a big boost and caused a 14-point swing. All of a sudden, in the course of about four minutes, we went from being down by three touchdowns to being down by just one.

It was wild in our locker room at half time. We couldn't wait to get back out onto the field because we knew we got the ball first. We knew that if we scored, we were back in a 0–0 game. Shula didn't say anything in the locker room except: "When we get the ball—let's tie it up." He knew the emotion was so high that he didn't have to get anybody pumped up. You felt the electricity in our locker room. We were ready to go out and play. I'd been on the other end of games like that, and I knew that the Chargers, in their locker room, were saying, "Wow—how did that happen?" It had to be a very disheartening half time for them.

Starting the second half, the momentum had definitely changed. We were getting the ball back and starting all over again. Four minutes and ten seconds into the third quarter, the horrible hankies were all over the place. Fans were going wild. It was loud out there, and it got even louder. I hit Joe Rose on a 15-yard pass, and he went in for the touchdown, and the score was tied. That capped a 74-yard drive in eight plays. The Chargers came back and took the lead at the 10:45 mark when Fouts hit Winslow with a 25-yard pass. It was like an air show. On the sixth play of a drive that went 83 yards, I connected with Bruce Hardy on a 50-yard touchdown pass. Uwe von Schamann's extra point tied the score at 31.

Everyone knew a lot of big numbers were being put up on both sides, but no one really knew exactly what they were. That was for the newspaper guys to report in the papers the next day. The only number at that point that I was concerned about was the fact that we were tied. So to me, the score was zero to zero.

We actually took the lead in the game starting off the fourth quarter on a 12-yard run by Tony Nathan. That was just unbelievable. In two quarters we had scored 38 points. But Fouts drove them 82 yards in the fourth quarter and hit James Brooks with a touchdown pass to tie the game with just 58 seconds to go in regulation time.

We thought we had it won four minutes before. Now with Uwe von Schamann, an excellent kicker who had made 18 of his last 20 attempts, we thought we had it won again. We thought that his 43-yard kick was going to be the last play of the game. But he hit the ball fat, the sand flew, the kick was low, and it was blocked by Kellen Winslow, who usually didn't play on the field-goal blocking unit.

"That was the biggest thrill of my life," Kellen said later. "I felt like I scored three touchdowns."

What could you do?

In overtime, we had a chance to win early. Uwe was on the spot again, trying a field goal from 34 yards out. But he hit the ball low, and it was blocked by defensive end Leroy Jones.

It was unbelievable. It seemed that nobody wanted to win the game. That made it three field goal attempts missed in a row. Uwe had missed two, and Rolf Benirschke of the Chargers had missed a 27-yard attempt at the beginning of the overtime.

But Rolf didn't miss his second try. He kicked a 29-yarder at the 13-minute 52-second mark, and San Diego won the game, 41–38.

Dan Fouts, Charger quarterback, completed 33 of 53 passes for 433 yards, a league play-off record. He also threw for three touchdowns. But the real star of the game was Kellen Winslow, who caught 13 passes, a play-off record, for 166 yards. Winslow was heroic out there. He had a pinched nerve in his left shoulder that got aggravated each time somebody ran into him. He had cramps in his back and legs. He was cut on his lip, and his left eye was swollen. And it seemed every chance he had, he was taking a long drag on the oxygen tank because of the heat. The guy was something else.

I wound up completing 29 of 43 passes for 403 yards and four touchdowns. Everybody said it was a dream game for me, but it wasn't. For it to have been a dream, we would have had to have won by a field goal 41–38 and not lost.

Don Coryell, the Charger coach, said: "I have coached for 32 years. And this was tremendous. There has never been a game like this. It was probably the most exciting game in pro football history."

But the *Miami Herald* headline the next day summed it up best: "The Miracle That Died."

Through my time in the league I was exposed to a lot of pressure situations. But the most nut-cutting times were during the players' strikes. Back in 1974, Joe Robbie had this to say about the NFL Players Association strike: "This is the first time in the history of labor negotiations that $100,000 players are driving Mark IVs or Cadillacs to the picket line."

In 1982, Russell Baker wrote in *The New York Times*: "News that a strike of football players might wipe out the entire football season left me positively pleased. Didn't we just have a football season a few weeks ago?"

In 1987, Charles Jackson, who was a replacement defensive back for the Redskins, came up with a beauty. "We are the official Washington Redskins. We represent the entire state of Washington."

Those kind of comments have demeaned the honest efforts of the Players Association and the guys who have put their careers and their reputations on the line to strike for better conditions in the National Football League. No one has enjoyed being involved in strikes. I've been through three of them, and the scars are still there. But going up against the monopoly that is the League with all its media influence, there hasn't been any other way. I find it hard to believe Pete Rozelle couldn't have avoided those strikes. But on second thought, he had to let them happen. The National Football League Commissioner is paid by management. Rozelle was commissioner for thirty years. And he made around $500,000 per year. So he wasn't a guy who was going to ever bite the hand that fed him. That ugly job was reserved for the players. It made for some rip-roaring, ball-breaking times.

The 1982 preseason, with a strike pending, was tension-filled. All the NFL players in favor of going out wanted to show their unity. We figured shaking hands before games with the opposition was as good a way as any to do that. But Don Shula said he didn't want anyone out there shaking hands. He claimed doing that was bullshit. He felt it was a slap in his face to go out and shake hands with the opposition when we're supposed to be beating the shit out of them five minutes later.

But we did it anyway. The fans didn't like it and booed to show us, but, as union members, we stuck to our guns. I wonder why. There were just a few guys intimidated enough by Shula into not doing it—five rookies and Bob Kuechenberg. A guard out of Notre Dame, Kuch was one of the strongest guys I ever played with. His limbs were just like steel rods. In

1970, he came to Miami as a free agent and was on the taxi squad and did not play. But he worked himself into a football player; he made himself great. By 1982, Kuechenberg had everything going his way. He was the team captain and respected by everyone.

When all the preparations for the strike were getting under way with the representatives from the NFL Players Association, Kuechenberg stood up to speak at a team player meeting. "Whatever we do," he said, "let's do it together."

The season got under way. We beat the Jets on September 12 in New York, 45–28. Then we beat the Baltimore Colts in Miami on September 19, 24–10. And then the strike was on.

Bob Kuechenberg was the only Miami Dolphin player to cross the line, to go into the locker room, to practice. He said he had a personal services deal with Joe Robbie that obliged him to do this. They ran a picture of Kuch in the *Miami News* with the caption "The Lone Wolf." And that picture was on Joe Robbie's wall until his dying day.

After three or four days, he came out with the so-called Kuechenberg Plan. For the postseason, the head coach would get a full share of the money and assistant coaches would only get half. That plan was a joke to some people but not to John Sandusky, our offensive line coach. He was dead serious.

Kuechenberg was in the whirlpool getting his stimulation when John Sandusky stumbled onto him. And John just reamed Kuechenberg's ass up and down.

He screamed at Kuechenberg and told him in no uncertain terms what he thought of his so-called

Kuechenberg Plan. Sandusky was furious because the plan would give him only half the money he was supposed to get. John had a way with words and there was absolutely no way to mistake how he felt about the whole thing.

After about a week, there was a lockout. No one got paid—not even Kuechenberg. There were no games, no advertising. The NFL made nothing.

They called it a lockout. I call it a strike. And it dragged on and on. Doug Dieken, the Browns' player rep, reported on meeting with the commissioner's office: "The best thing that came out of it was that they told us not to steal the ashtrays." That gave everyone a feeling of the tone of the times.

Don Shula outwardly was not for the strike. Inwardly, he wanted to get the show to go on, wanted his players there, wanted his team to play.

We had a good veteran nucleus of players on the Dolphins, and we all stayed together as a team. We had our first meetings at Costa Del Sol, a golf course I used to work at. We organized our practice and meeting schedules there. We had it much better than the teams up north, because the weather turned bad for them, and there were limited places they could go. In Florida, we had good weather and worked out at Miami Dade Community College, the North Campus. We had to sign waivers that if anyone was injured, we were on our own.

Out of 45 to 47 guys on the roster, we had 37 or 38 a day coming down for the workouts. We ran our gassers, did our stretching, we did pat and go. There were individual passing drills for the quarterbacks and the wide receivers, one-on-one coverage, for full-team defensive line against full-team offensive line. The Blackwood brothers in the secondary called the defensive coverages. I was calling the plays on the other side. Nat Moore worked with the receivers. And after every practice, we sat down and talked about what was going on in the strike. It was a tough time for everyone, and a lot of money was lost, but the work put in by guys like Nat Moore and myself—making the phone calls, organizing the meetings and practices, seeing there was money lent back and forth to help people out—made it easier for all of us.

There was always so much misinformation going around about the strike and the demands of the union and the offers of the owners. Some guy would say, "I think free agency should be granted to a player in his fifth year."

I'd ask, "What year are you in?"

"I'm in my fifth."

Another guy would say: "I think a seven-year guy should have free agency."

"What year are you in?" I'd ask.

"I'm in my seventh."

That was the way it went. Lots of frustrations, mixed-up feelings, but also some laughs.

One of the highlights of that strike was a game played in RFK Stadium in Washington, D.C., by the striking NFL players. In back of the whole deal was Ted Turner, who was trying to get the opportunity to televise games in the NFL. Each guy was paid $2,500 out of the NFL Players Association fund. We had some great players. On my side, the wide receivers were Wesley

Walker, Stanley Morgan, Ray Butler, and Nat Moore. John Riggins and Lee Roy Selmon played. In addition to Nat Moore and myself, other Dolphins who played were Dwight Stephenson, Ed Newman, Doug Betters, and Tony Nathan. The head coach of our team was Tom Matte, and the head coach on the other side was Chris Hanburger from the Redskins.

Nobody wanted to hurt anybody, so there wasn't a lot of physical craziness, but there was enthusiasm and a spirit of togetherness. Steve Grogan was the other quarterback on my team. Since I had only had a chance to get in 45 minutes of practice with the team before the game, Grogan played the first half. I played the third quarter huffing and puffing, and we flipped a dime for the fourth quarter. I called heads, and it came out tails, and I played.

We didn't have a whole lot of people in the stands, but we had a lot of fun playing. My number was 17; our uniforms were patchwork scraped up here and there from companies that donated gear. Everybody was pretty happy the way the game turned out. The final score was 25–23, or something, very close. After the game, Ted Turner was in the locker room drinking beer with all of us. He said he was backing the strike all the way because the NFL tried to screw him, too, by shutting him out of getting games to televise. He must have lost at least a million dollars on that game itself. But Ted Turner persevered. As we all know, today his ESPN network does quite a few NFL games a year.

After that game was on TV, the guys on the Dolphins who had been doubters were no longer on the fence. They became believers in the strike, seeing how everyone from different teams all over the league was together. On November 21, the strike was finally settled.

Bob Kuechenberg came back in with the rest of us. But he was tarnished. He lasted a couple of more years with the Dolphins, but that Lone Wolf stuff and crossing the line stuck with him, alienating him from a lot of people. He didn't have a lot of friends on the Dolphins his last years. The rest of the players were always talking about how he got the same money we did from the owners, but we stayed out and put our jobs on the line and fought for it. And that left a bitter taste in a lot of people's mouths.

Guys made a lot of jokes about the strike. "One good thing came out of it," Matt Cavanaugh, who was then the New England Patriots' quarterback, said. "My wife's pregnant."

Jokes aside, it was a long, bitter strike, and it was good to be back playing in the National Football League again. We had missed a bunch of games, being out a total of fifty-seven days. But the togetherness of the Dolphins, the workouts every day, made us a tougher team. When the season resumed, we played against teams that we knew had better talent than us and we beat them. Those teams had been broken up during the strike, gone home, got other jobs, what have you. It had been a "You call me when we're going back to work" with most teams.

In 1982, Mark Duper out of NW Louisiana State was picked number two by the Dolphins in the draft. A guy from the backwoods of Louisiana, he liked the action in Miami, still does. Mark was always a nice guy to get along with.

Dupe is very fast, but the fastest guy I ever saw in my life was Ray Robinson, signed as a free agent in 1973 or 1974. He helped set a world record at Florida A & M. This guy could really fly, but he was a frail type who didn't like coming over the middle. I'm not sure that Dupe could run with him, because Robinson was 4.2 and a little change for the 40 running on grass. But if they ever would have competed, it would have been a close race.

Rich Diana, a fullback out of Yale, a really bright guy, was also picked by the Dolphins in 1982. We always had our share of brainy types like Rich and Doug Swift out of Amherst and Gary Fencik in 1976 from Yale. Shula admitted to me that he had many sleepless nights deciding between keeping Fencik or Tim Foley. He let Gary get away, and as we all know, he became an All-Pro player with the Chicago Bears.

The whole 1982 season Bob Griese and I were on the scene for the Dolphins as two figures somehow misplaced. Bob had one year left on his contract and honored it by coaching. But Bob was not too happy about it all. "Don," he told me with a straight face, "if you ever want to drop off the face of the earth, be an assistant coach." I thought that was a very interesting statement.

I was misplaced as a backup to Woodley, a savior, whatever you want to call it. Shula said I played a vital role on the team, that I was going to get a full-fledged shot as a starting quarterback. But none of that came to be.

One of the most memorable games of 1982 was on December 12 against New England. The field conditions were near unbearable—frigid, cold, brutal, not fit for man nor beast. No one could move the football or get any kind of offense mounted. At one point we tried a field goal, but Uwe Von Schamman fell flat on his ass as he tried to kick it. Late in the game the Patriots lined up for a field goal try of their own. Some guy came out onto the field with a snowplow with a brush on it. We all thought he was coming out there to clear off the lines for the referees. But he was out there to clear a path for New England to attempt the field goal! Their kicker was John Smith, from England. The kick went up—good! We lost the game 3–0. Shula was so cold that he stood there looking like a frozen statue. The fans went crazy. We found out later that the guy with the snowplow was a convict who worked at the stadium as part of a work-release program. He became a big hero in New England and that bizarre game would forever be remembered as the "Snowplow Game."

That was only our second loss in nine games in the strike-shortened 1982 season. In the play-offs we marched through, beating New England, San Diego, and then the Jets, 14–0. That was the A. J. Duhe game, where he intercepted three balls, one for a touchdown. The Jet coach Walt Michaels claimed we hadn't put the tarp down when it had rained before the game and that gave us an edge. In reality, we just outplayed them.

The 1983 Super Bowl was a matchup of the Killer Bees of Miami against the Hogs of Washington. Miami's Killer Bees picked up their nickname because six of our defenders had last names beginning with "B." The Hogs were a big power-blocking line who got down and dirty.

The game was played before 103,677 in Pasadena's

Rose Bowl—the largest crowd a Miami Dolphins team ever played in front of.

David Woodley had 97 yards passing in the first half. Most of the yardage came on a little pass to Jimmy Cefalo that he just grabbed and took off on. He scored a touchdown. Just near the end of the first half, one of the better-looking plays, but one of the worst plays that could have happened to us, took place. Fulton Walker returned a Washington kickoff 98 yards for a touchdown. If that had not happened, I would have started at quarterback for the second half instead of David Woodley. But with us being ahead, he went in.

We were totally shut down in the second half. Woodley was 0 for 8. We managed just two first downs and gained only 34 yards. Washington scored 21 points. Riggins had himself a game rushing the football.

With seven minutes and something left in the fourth quarter, Shula told me to warm up. But by the time I got out there, the Redskins had used up the clock and scored another touchdown. I finally entered the game with a minute something left and there wasn't much I could do. We lost the game 27–17. My mother and father were at the game, and after it was over, Shula apologized to my father for not getting me into the game sooner. But how could Shula know that the Redskins would control the ball as long as they did and totally dominate things? So it was a nice gesture to my father on Shula's part.

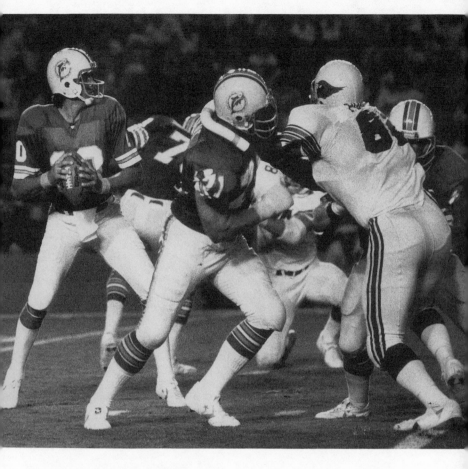

Aug. 5, 1978: In a preseason game against the St. Louis Cardinals, Don Strock (10) gets ready to pass.

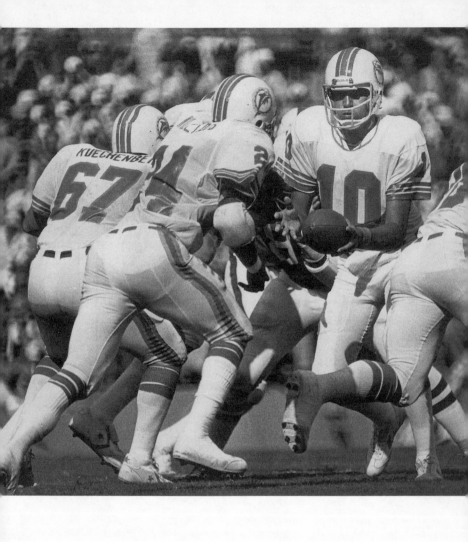

(Opposite) Aug. 17, 1978: In preseason play against the Buffalo Bills, Don Strock (10) hands off to Delvin Williams (24).

(Below) Dec. 12, 1978: Against the Oakland Raiders, Don Strock (10) holds for Garo Yepremian (1) for an extra-point kick after a touchdown.

(Above) Dec. 15, 1979: Don Strock (10) hands off to Larry Csonka (38) in the Csonk's final regular season NFL game, played against the New York Jets.

(Right) Aug. 14, 1982: With a strike pending, Dolphins and Washington Redskins players shake hands before a preseason game in a show of unity.

Dec. 12, 1982: Don Strock and Uwe Von Schamann (5) celebrate Uwe's winning field goal against the New York Jets.

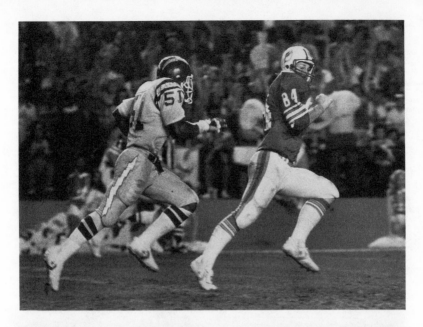

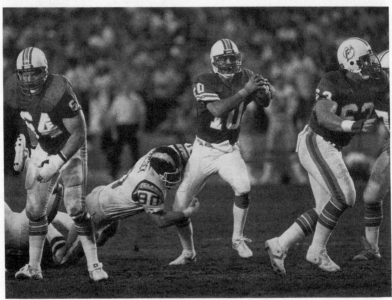

Jan. 2, 1982: *(Top)* In the playoff game against San Diego, Bruce Hardy (84) runs for a touchdown on a 50-yard pass from Don Strock. *(Bottom)* Strock (10) scrambles to get off a pass. Strock, who entered the game in the second quarter, completed 29 of 43 passes for 403 yards and four touchdowns. *(Opposite)* In overtime Strock (10) looks on in disbelief as Uwe Von Schamann (5) misses a possible game-winning field goal.

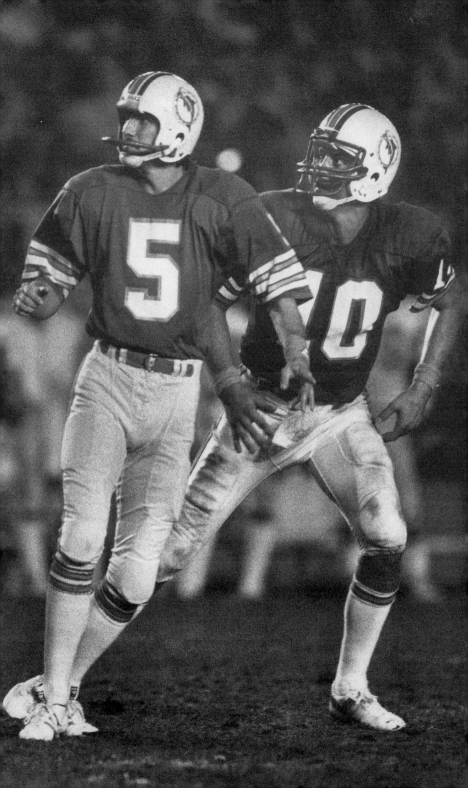

Dec. 16, 1983: *(Above)* Playing against the New York Jets in the final game of the season, Don Strock (10) throws a pass to Bruce Hardy. *(Opposite)* Shaken up by the New York Jets defense, Strock (10) comes off the field with the team doctor and a trainer.

Nov. 4, 1984: Nat Moore's (89) famous "helicopter" spin in a game against the New York Jets.

Nov. 11, 1984: Doug Bettors (75) blocks a field goal attempt by the Philadelphia Eagles to seal a 24-23 victory.

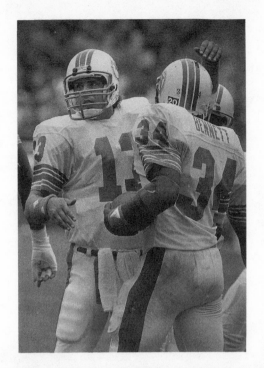

Nov. 18, 1984: *(Left)* Dan Marino (13) celebrates a touchdown pass to Woody Bennett (34) in a game against the San Diego Chargers. *(Below)* Marino throws another touchdown pass against San Diego, this time to Mark Clayton. In this game, Marino threw his 37th touchdown pass of the season, breaking the record held by Y.A. Tittle and George Blanda.

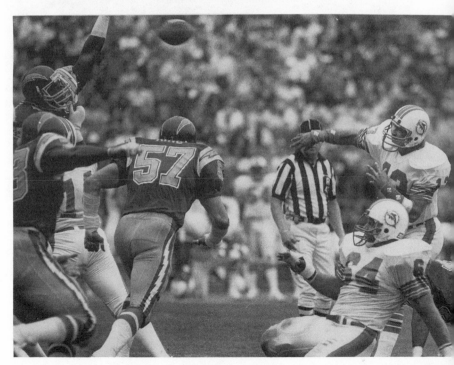

Dec. 2, 1985: *(Above)* Mark Duper (85) and Mark Clayton (83) celebrate after the Dolphin victory over the previously undefeated Chicago Bears. *(Opposite)* Dan Marino (13) drops back to pass.

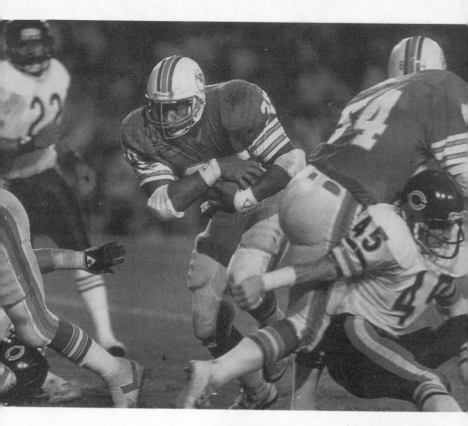

(Above) Dec. 2, 1985: Ron Davenport (30) scores a touchdown in the Chicago Bears' only loss of the season.

(Right) Jan. 1, 1985: Joe Robbie, the late owner of the Miami Dolphins, watches the action in Super Bowl XIX, which the Dolphins lost to the San Francisco 49ers, 38-16, at the Stanford Stadium.

Sept. 21, 1986: Mark Clayton (83) makes a pass reception against the New York Jets.

Sept. 13, 1987: Don Strock (10) punts in the rain against the New England Patriots.

(Above) Nov. 29, 1987: From left to right, defensive lineman Mark Dennis, Dolphins head coach Don Shula, Dan Marino, and Don Strock on the side-lines in a game against the Buffalo Bills.

(Left) Dec. 2, 1987: Don Strock and Don Shula discuss strategy in a game against the Buffalo Bills.

Dec. 12, 1988: Don Strock (12), quarterbacking for the Cleveland Browns, in his "homecoming" game against the Dolphins in Miami.

BEHIND CLOSED DOORS

BEING a member of a National Football League team isn't exactly like hanging out in summer camp. But there are certain similarities—a bunch of guys from different backgrounds in close proximity with time on their hands. Mix that in with the constant pressure of the game, the drive to succeed, different egos, reputations, needs, desires, attitudes toward life and career, and we can begin.

Today, players wearing earrings is a standard thing all over the NFL. Dangling, hanging, inset, insert, reversed, upside down, diamonds, gold stars ... they've got it, the whole nine yards. We on the Dolphins never had a whole lot of earring wearers until recent years. I always said you could judge the quality of a team by how many earrings you could count on their players. Now, with so many wearing earrings, you can judge the quality of a football team by how many of the players aren't wearing earrings.

The first guy to get into earrings on Miami in a serious way was Marv Fleming. He was a guy with all those Super Bowl rings, and I guess he spent a lot of time thinking about what he could do with them. He got an idea. Removing one of the diamonds from a ring, he had a diamond earring made up special for his use. One day Marv came into the clubhouse all bright and beaming, puffed up and proud, sporting that diamond earring. Then he runs into Shula.

"Coach, you notice anything different about me?"

"Yeah," Shula says without any emotion at all. "Where's your other earring?"

The kind of car a player drives is a big deal. Cars are definitely status symbols. We had players making $60,000 and driving $30,000 cars. The cars weren't paid for, but the guys were driving them and paying through the nose to pay them off.

Mercury Morris loved fancy cars. He changed on and off driving them the way guys change into different suits. Mark Duper bought a Rolls Royce from Norman Braman, the owner of the Philadelphia Eagles, who is a big car dealer in Florida. Dupe got the car for nothing down and endless payments. But he didn't have that car for very long. By the time he had paid about $125,000 on it, he traded it in for two other cars. One was a speedy little sports car and the other one was another elegant luxury car.

The Dolphin parking lot was always a who's who of the newest, the sleekest, the sexiest, the most expensive cars. And most of them were loaded with frills. The guys who drove them were proud of those machines. And sometimes they weren't.

One defensive back had a little two-seater. It was a ball-buster for him getting in and out of that thing, but he managed somehow. The car cost $98,000 and he was anxious to show it off with him in it. After one game he was trying to back it out of his spot in the parking lot, and that sucker stalled four times. Finally, it sputtered and chugged away. I always wondered how far he got.

Hugh Green, a lover of fast cars if there ever was one, always bragged about his. But he met his match in Mark Duper. "I'll tell you what," Mark said. "I'll take my car and whip your ass. I'll race you from Miami to Florida [sic]!"

There was always a lot of security around those high-priced cars, so no one was really too concerned about theirs being stolen. But petty theft was always part of the scene.

Towels, tee shirts, jocks, shorts, shirts—that kind of stuff was always disappearing from the lockers in the training camp and even during the season. The kind of soap we got in camp was an inferior version of Fels Naphtha. Guys would take bars by the carload to use in their homes. It was ridiculous.

The toilet paper that was issued was like wax paper and would hurt your ass when you used it. Yet, about twenty rolls of that stuff would be used up or disappear every couple of days. I knew a lot of guys were full of shit, but that was too much.

The only way some of that petty stealing was able to be dealt with was the once-a-week training camp sweeps by the equipment manager and his assistant. When we were out on the practice field, they'd go into the dorms and rummage through the rooms and collect and cart away batches of towels, shorts, shirts, soap, and toilet paper. I'm sure the guys who planned on taking the stuff never missed it.

Weigh-ins were always big-time stuff with the Dolphins. Coach Shula and his staff always took this procedure very seriously—weigh-ins were treated like a ritual. Weigh-ins were mandatory every Thursday morning. There was an early one at 7:30 and a later one at 9:15, right before you went into a meeting, and players who didn't make the weight were fined twenty-five dollars a pound per day. For some of those horses, that could prove to be pretty expensive. Darryl Carlton came to the training camp so overweight that by the time he made weight after a week or so, he had piled up $1,250 in fines. So guys would go to great lengths to make weight.

Those who were under would drink water or Gatorade, eat doughnuts or an enormous country breakfast, or do any of a number of other things to get their weight up. Guys who were over would sweat it out, stop eating, piss like crazy, do whatever gyrations they could to imbalance the scale and make the weight. Once, they found some coins under the scale and the word went out and there was a big commotion that the players were trying to make fools of themselves and the organization.

For several years we were asked to weigh in the day after Thanksgiving. Talk about tough! After eating those big holiday meals, everybody came back weighing at least five or six pounds more. Some guys were even ten to fifteen pounds up in their weight—that was a lot of turkey.

There was such a big fuss made about the extra weight that it seemed that if you fumbled or threw an interception it was not nearly as bad as being over-weight. Weight, the right playing weight, was a fixa-tion, a fetish, a pain in the ass.

One year the team doctors had us lie face-down in water with weights attached to us. The idea was for the players to stick their head in the water and blow. There was a gadget hooked on to each of us that was supposed to register a certain number—the right playing weight. Well, we lay down, we blew and we sank.

Results? Results were ridiculous. One of our offensive lineman had an assigned playing weight of 305, but the water test registered him in at 255 as optimum weight. It wasted a lot of time and guys got pretty wet, but after a while they dropped those water tests.

The next year some bright person came up with the idea of using calipers. They attached electrodes around our big toes, and that was supposed to be the key to giving the precise readout as to how much we should weigh. Talk about time-consuming—the damn thing took a whole morning and part of an afternoon to get it done on all the players and the coaches on the Dolphins.

When the test results came back, there were a lot of shockers. Mine said I was supposed to weigh between 226 and 232 pounds. My assigned playing weight was 224, and I had been begging for a couple of extra pounds to be assigned to me for the weigh-in. So when I got that test result I was damn happy.

But that was not the case with Don Shula. The claim that Shula made was that he weighed 214—probably it was a little more than that. One of our offensive line coaches, John Sandusky, was very heavy at the time. He had to have weighed around 300 pounds. Anyway Shula came over to me and was furious.

He told me he didn't think the tests were worth anything. When I asked him what he meant by that he mentioned how John Sandusky was going around beaming because the tests showed Shula had more body fat than Sandusky. There was no way that was true, Shula said. According to Shula, these tests were out, but something new—a better way—would be found.

Next Monday we were doing the caliper test again. Only this time the calipers were not on our toes—they were attached to our sides. Then water test that was once given up as horseshit came back into use. Things, as you can see, went around and around in circles.

But one of our defensive ends, Doug Betters, had learned something about the water test the first time around. Into the water he goes with a 5-pound weight in one hand and a 2.5-pound weight in the other. He puts the weights into his trunks, and he's there treading away in the water. And they're telling him, "Blow it out. Blow it all out!"

The more you had on you, the more the test showed you were supposed to weigh, so Betters, who was supposed to weigh 265, had a few extra pounds to play around with.

The Dallas Cowboys received a lot of publicity for all

of their tests and workouts and scientific approaches to conditioning. We had that stuff, too. But as you can see, what we had was primitive stuff, nutso stuff.

The "blue mark" was sort of the code word for excellence in speed and dexterity. We were tested, tested, and rewarded with a blue mark, like an "A" in school.

They had you jump straight up. If you jumped over 36 inches, they gave you a blue mark. If you ran 6½ laps in 12 minutes, you got a blue mark. Then there was the leapfrog. If you jumped twice from standing position, they would measure it. If you went over 10 feet, you got a blue mark.

We'd run shuttles—the 40-yard dash. The quarterbacks would do them first. They should have used an egg timer for me—that was how fast I was. There was a time registered for 20 yards and another for 40 yards. If you ran under 4.6 or 4.5 seconds for 40 yards, you got a blue mark. It depended on what position you played.

There were 5-yard shuttles. There were 15-yard shuttles. We were shuttled all over the place. We'd have practices for about an hour, and then there was the 12-minute run. We were running all over the place.

No one who received blue marks in every shuttle or run ever made the Miami Dolphins. These were guys with great speed, dexterity, but somehow they couldn't play football. Everybody on the team knew about the legend of the blue marks.

Fresh meat, new guys, would come in anxious to do well and show off their ability. "Whatever you do," we'd tell them, "don't get too many blue marks."

They looked at us as if we were crazy.

The 12-minute run would be set to start. "Whatever you do," the veterans would yell out to the new blood, "don't win this race. It's the kiss of death."

They didn't believe us.

The announcement would come out: "Johnny Smith just set a new record for the 12-minute run."

And we veterans would groan. "See you later, Johnny."

Behind closed doors all kinds of things go on. There are orders to do this, eat that, watch him, look in. What I learned most of all was to listen to my own body and not to what someone else was telling me to do with it. Quarterbacks and receivers need to be able to bend and move. Most of all, they don't need to be all built up. Richard Todd, who was with the Jets, was a quarterback who was a weightlifter and got all built up and he paid the price. He broke into pieces when he played.

What I realized was that the Nautilus for tightness was most important for me. I didn't need to do a whole lot of bench presses and chins.

Bruce Hardy and I used to walk out of the weight room and report to a part-time trainer. As Bruce and I recall it, the dialogue went something like this. "Partner, we did six leg presses, fifteen dips, five chins."

"I can't write that down."

"Why not?"

"I watched and you guys hardly did any of those things."

"You're right," I tell him. "And you know what? I'm not going to do any of that stuff."

"You got to do it, you guys." Now he's whining.

"I tell you what," I give him the big smile. "You put down that we did nothing if you want."

He says, "What am I going to show Coach Shula?"

"Show him I did none of that."

"I can't do that. He told me to get everyone down by noon today."

"Okay, get us down, 6–15–5 . . ."

So he makes a face and starts walking away. Bruce and I weren't concerned at all because we knew that eventually he would do it.

Another big deal was the contest we conducted on the Dolphins at the start of each season to pick the National Football League's "Mr. All Ugly." There was always time to kill in the locker room and a natural curiosity about who was on the different rosters of the other teams. So a bunch of us would go looking through programs and guides, searching out our selections. A player on the Cincinnati Bengals won the "Mr. All Ugly" award five or six years running. And believe me that was quite an accomplishment because he always had a lot of stiff competition. And I do mean stiff.

The arrival of mail was another thing that made for some interesting times. You never knew what you were getting but we got a lot—postcards, packages, Federal Express, coupons, prizes, shopping bags, flowers. All the mail was dispersed by uniform number. You'd open an envelope and there'd be a note from some kid in Montana or Kansas wanting your autograph. That was standard stuff. Or there'd be all those repeat letters from people who had been following your career since it began way back in college. We called those letters "the regulars."

There were also "irregulars," and those were the prize pieces of correspondence. Those were generally letters sent in by girls posing in their bra and panties and promising a good time for one and all. Sometimes the girls didn't even have a bra and panties on. For some they should have kept their clothes on, because we wound up looking over some mean-looking bodies. Along with the photographs there were always letters included—some of them perfumed, most of them usually ending with the words: "Give me a call," or "I can't wait."

If someone got something that was especially hot, that letter and picture were pinned up on the bulletin board for everyone to enjoy. And there were always screams like "Hot stuff," "Way to go," "Give her a call."

The locker room was also a place that strange visitors somehow found their way into despite all the security precautions. There was the standard amount of jock-strap salesmen, athletic gear peddlers, people who wanted to be your new agent, autograph seekers. But that was tame stuff compared with the couple of disgruntled fans who came in one day looking to pick a fight. They were disposed of quickly.

There were also invited guests for when a player had a birthday or some other special day. That's when beauty queen type girls would suddenly appear.

One of the most exciting visitors we ever had come in behind closed doors was a girl arranged for by Mark Duper for Nat Moore's birthday. This wasn't the first time it happened. Girls being brought in for birthdays and special occasions for guys happened many times. It was a regular ritual in the locker room.

Nat looked forward to his birthday present. He was not only a fun-loving guy but also one of the all-time Dolphin greats. What a tremendous receiver he was, with 500 some catches. As a matter of fact, I threw him his 500th ball. Nat played all kinds of positions— tight end, running back, both receivers. He returned punts and kickoffs. And he had all those deceptive moves.

The girl that was brought in to entertain had all the moves, too. A lot of those moves most of us had never seen done just that way before. But she attracted a crowd dancing around in the executive locker room area, way in the back. Guys were back there cheering her on and watching her strut her stuff to the beat of some very loud music.

Nat sat comfortably on a chair while she danced around him like a belly dancer. Since he was supposed to be the object of her affection or attention or act or whatever you want to call it, she showed she cared by putting her underwear around his neck and head. I can't say that Nat was pleased to have that silky stuff there, but he didn't run away from it.

Don Shula must have heard the commotion because

we heard him bellow to Bobby Monica, our equipment guy, "Find out what the hell is going on back there!"

Bobby tried his best, but there was such a mob of big bodies watching that girl gyrate that he couldn't make it through. His effort did, however, make most of the guys scatter because we all knew what was coming down.

Shula started to make his way through. Bruce Hardy caught sight of him. Then in full pads Bruce jumped into the shower. He didn't want any trouble.

Nat Moore, Dan Marino, and I were stuck all the way in the back and couldn't get out. I wouldn't say we were trapped; there just wasn't too much room to maneuver. I'm not so sure that Nat Moore was too anxious to leave anyway.

Shula came charging in. "You guys are testing me, dammit." I guess he thought that all that was going on was a lot of partying and loud music. But then his demeanor changed as he came up closer and caught a good look at the girl bumping away. "Get your clothes on and get the hell out of here!" Shula was livid.

The girl had aplomb—I think that means grace under pressure. She gave Shula a great big smile and said: "You don't mind if I finish my dance, do you?"

Clothes on, clothes off, brings me to another story. It seemed that whenever there was a guy with no clothes on, there was one player who was always on the spot with his eyes wide open. One time Manny Fernandez was showering. The guy was ogling. Maybe it was one ogle too many for Manny.

"You asshole!" was how Manny began. He had a way with words. "What the fuck are you looking at?"

"Nothing."

"Don't be insulting," Manny said. "Stay the fuck away from me, you asshole."

The guy didn't last too long before Shula cut him from the team. I can't say he was gay, but he sure loved to look.

Talk about looking. I know the women's libbers won't like this, but let's talk about one aspect of the locker room—what some people call the "lockerroom watchers." As far as I am concerned, the locker room with a bunch of undressed or half-dressed males is no place for a woman. As a man in a locker room with other guys, I never bothered to look, but I often wondered if I was in a room with a bunch of women what I would do. It's only human nature. I'd probably look. So I wonder if any of the women reporters, or what have you, sneak a peak.

For a time there on the Dolphins they gave us robes with our numbers on them. We were told to cover up and wear those robes. Some guys wore them and some didn't, and most times with forty-five guys heading to the shower at the same time, there were robes thrown all over the place. And maybe sometimes the women reporters were sneaking a peek. With some guys there was a lot to look at.

Most guy's wives wouldn't want to be in the locker room after a game when players are showering or walking around half naked. But the issue is like putting your eyes onto things where they don't belong. It can only cause trouble. And it does.

In October 1990 Lisa Olson, a reporter for the *Boston Herald*, charged some New England Patriot players with sexual harassment. A week or so after she did that, Commissioner Paul Tagliabue fined Cincy coach Sam Wyche one seventeenth of his salary for not allowing locker room access to Denise Tom of *USA Today*. The fine was $27,941—the largest ever given out to any player or coach in NFL history. Talk about the punishment fitting the crime, talk about extreme. In my view, if there are no male or female reporters in a women's tennis locker room, if you're going to be fair to all, there should be no female or male reporters in NFL locker rooms because the way things now exist is no good.

In theory the way that it's supposed to work is that reporters are scheduled to go into the coaches' area first for a statement. Then the reporters are supposed to go to the players. But a lot of them never wind up doing that. They go right to the players. And just after the heat of the battle with adrenaline still flowing, players sometimes say a lot of things that they regret the following day. Also it's awfully difficult to get undressed in front of your locker when women or men are there watching and pumping you for quotes. You're talking about a gladiator's uniform being torn off and all of a sudden they're there in your face with microphones, note pads, whatever, standing in your way. For many years it was very hard for me to even get to my locker, which was right next to Bob Griese's or Dan Marino's. I'd be coming out of the shower and there was such a mob around my locker that I couldn't even get my clothes out.

The solution to the whole problem that would be fair for everyone is to set up a conference room in all NFL stadiums. A player could then be escorted fully dressed or with shorts on by a club representative to that room for an interview with reporters—men and women. That would be good for everyone—the players and the press, male and female. And behind closed doors would really be what it's meant to be—behind closed doors.

THE ENDING YEARS: 1983–1987

IN January of 1983, the first pick in the draft for the Dolphins was Dan Marino, quarterback. Many people interpreted that as a message to everyone as to how far Miami management felt David Woodley could take them. Dan was selected number 27 in the draft—the fifth quarterback taken, after John Elway, Todd Blackledge, Tony Eason, Ken O'Brien.

To this day people wonder, after seeing all that Dan Marino has accomplished, how he could have been selected behind those other quarterbacks. Well, there were some questions about him. He had been a big star at the University of Pittsburgh, received a lot of media exposure playing in a major college football program. But some complained that he seemed to carry himself with a kind of macho image, that he had an attitude problem. Others whispered that he had a drug problem—those were just whispers, but they had an effect. The most damning thing against him was that he didn't have a good senior year. But had those critics looked more closely they would have realized that in Dan's senior year on the playing field, problems came about because he was trying too hard, trying to carry his Pitt team.

Today Don Shula looks like a genius for making Dan Marino Miami's top pick. But the credit really goes to head scout Chuck Connor, who talked Shula into picking Dan. Chuck sold his soul to get it done, but he doesn't always get the credit for it.

Others who joined the Dolphins in 1983 included punter Reggie Roby out of Iowa, a number 7 pick, and Mark Clayton. Reggie is a meek and quiet 260-pounder with a great leg. Clayton, wide receiver out of Louisville, was pick number 8 for the Dolphins, but he was a steal. One of the best athletes in the game of football today, Mark had the record for 18 touchdown catches in a season. He's a piece of work out there.

With Dan Marino coming in and David Woodley still on the scene, it was common sense that I had to explore my options. I held out in 1983 and did a lot of talking to people in the USFL—the Memphis Showboats, Oklahoma Outlaws, Chicago Blitz. They all wanted to sign me. Finally, my agent Jerry Kapstein worked out an agreement with Joe Robbie.

On Labor Day 1983 at eight o'clock in the morning I got a phone call from Coach Shula. And, as I remember it, he says, "Get your ass in here and go through all the testing, and get to work."

I came back in after missing the first week and the first game. Shula welcomed me back: "It makes me want to vomit that you're being paid for the first game."

In the Dolphin depth chart Dan Marino was number

one at quarterback. I was number two. Woodley was third string, and Don Shula made the statement that David probably wouldn't be playing for Miami in the near future.

Unlike Woodley, Dan Marino wanted to learn from me, wanted to talk about everything, and we spent a lot of time together. We became very close friends—the rookie quarterback and the veteran backup.

Throughout my career I followed the same rituals. I always got my ankles taped by the head trainer the same way every game. I followed a set method for putting on my thigh pads, knee pads, socks. I always put my own jersey on and never let anyone help me.

Dan Marino was the opposite, sort of deciding what he was going to do as he was doing it. But he did have one superstition, one ritual—his jersey. And even if I was there tying my shoe, he would stand and wait for me to come over and pull his jersey on for him.

He wasn't the neatest guy in the world when he first started out, and a lot of the guys got on him his first couple of years with the Dolphins. I saw firsthand what got them a little irritated. Dan's locker was next to mine, and he had the sloppiest one I've ever seen. He'd just throw shoes and T-shirts here and there. So we finally decided to pay guys to straighten things up. That made a difference.

One of the more humbling experiences for me took place once when Dan and I, his wife Claire, and my wife Debby came into a restaurant and were waiting to be seated. "Oh," the maître d' said, "so nice to see you, Mr. Marino. And you've brought your parents with you tonight."

At that time I was getting gray hair and my wife Debby had premature gray hair. It was fact that I was Dan's backup for a time, but I never thought I was a father figure in his life. But he is like a brother to me. Our families are very close. His son Dano is our godson. Usually, every Sunday during the off-season when we're in town, we go up to the Marinos' house and have dinner and play with their kids, talk about life in general, watch golf or baseball or whatever's on and just relax.

Dan needs his times to relax. For every game the pressure is always on him. He wears braces on both legs, big rib pads and shoulder pads. It's time-consuming to put those things on. And then when he goes out on the field with all the stuff on, he looks like a gladiator. And that's exactly what he is.

In his 1983 rookie season Dan Marino played extremely well. But with three games left in the season, he twisted his knee against Houston. I ended up finishing the game, and we won. Then I played against Atlanta and was 18–22 for some 200 yards, and we won again. In the last game of the year, I played against the Jets and we won 34–14. That was a good day for Mark Duper, who caught four of my passes for 71 yards and became the first Dolphin receiver to go over the 1,000-yard mark in a single season. It was a good day for me, too, but I paid a price. Joe Klecko came busting in and rammed me, just ruining my ribs.

We came up against Seattle in the play-offs. Dan had the bad knee, and I had the bad ribs, so we didn't really have anybody who could step in and take over the team at quarterback. We lost 27–20. It was the end of a 12–4 season. I thought we could have gone farther in the play-offs, but injuries are also part of the story.

In 1984, David Woodley was traded to Pittsburgh. The last I heard about him was that David was selling jewelry for a local company in the Dolphins' parking lot.

In the 1984 draft Jackie Shipp, linebacker from Oklahoma, was the number one pick of the Dolphins. They traded up with Buffalo from a twenty-something pick to get to the thirteenth spot to get him. Shipp was given a signing bonus of $1.3 million. It was hard to believe. He had to relearn the passing game, because at Oklahoma they didn't throw the ball that much. Shipp never panned out with the Dolphins, went on to the Raiders and is no longer in the game. Buffalo ended up getting Greg Bell for their pick, and he turned out to be a pretty good runner. So you never know.

For example, in the 1984 draft Miami's eleventh pick was Bud Brown from Southern Mississippi. He's another of those examples of how you never know how good a guy is until he comes to the team. The Dolphins struck pay dirt with Bud, who proved to be a truly solid player.

The 1984 draft had other facets to it. Miami came up with one of the most screwed-up scenarios in their draft history that year. They gave a second-round 1985 pick for fullback Chuck Muncie, who came in all screwed up and failed his urine test. He was never to be heard of again.

Also, Miami brought in Rickey Young, a running back who was released by Minnesota. "Hell," one of my teammates said. "He's even dirtier than Muncie." The guy had called the shot. In the middle of Young's first workout, the doctor came out—"Failed urine test." Gone.

So for the second-round 1985 pick, since the Dolphins rejected Chuck Muncie, San Diego sent Pete Johnson to Miami to show good faith. Pete came in, played a bit, and then was gone. Later on he was indicted in Cincinnati for distribution of cocaine, but he was later acquitted.

It was a case of three dirty beauties in one trade!

The magic year for Dan Marino was 1984. With the kind of team we had, our defense played well, but was not that dominant. It was necessary for Dan to throw the ball a lot. Most of the scores in the games we played were big numbers—lots of points scored against us, lots of points scored by the Dolphins. The passing game was what made us go.

On November 11, 1984, in the closing minutes of our game against the Eagles, Doug Betters blocked Philadelphia's try for a point after touchdown to seal our 24–23 win. That victory gave us an 11–0 record and 16 straight regular season wins.

The following week the San Diego Chargers, with their high-powered offense, defeated us in overtime, 34–28, snapping our winning streak. We lost our second game of the season, 45–34, to the Raiders, In that game Dan threw his 37th touchdown pass of the season, breaking the NFL record of 36 held by Y. A. Tittle and George Blanda. And he wasn't done yet!

When the season came to an end, Dan had thrown 48 touchdown passes, 18 to Mark Clayton. He became the first National Football League quarterback to pass for over 5,000 yards in one season. He was picked as the AP NFL Most Valuable Player. He was the main reason the Dolphins had the best record in the American Football Conference, 14–2.

In the play-offs we blew past Seattle and Pittsburgh and breezed into Super Bowl XIX. Our opposition was the San Francisco 49ers, the first team to win 15 of 16 regular season games. They had ten players voted to the Pro Bowl, including all four starting defensive backs. So we knew we had our work cut out for us.

The Super Bowl was played against the 49ers before 84,000 in a foggy Stanford Stadium. The conditions were the worst I ever saw. We had makeshift locker rooms, a bullshit setup. You can bet they'll never have a Super Bowl Game there again.

We got off well in the game, scoring early, and then San Francisco went to a four-man line with their pass rushers in and stuffed our run. To their credit, San Fran had a great game plan. It was clear they were saying, if you're going to beat us, you're going to have to run the ball.

Miami always tried to establish the run. But we had Tony Nathan and not much else there for any power running of the ball. Nine of our 16 points came on field goals. We were just overwhelmed after scoring in that first drive of the game. We didn't score a point in the second half and lost the game 38–16.

The game was advertised as Dan Marino versus Joe Montana. But it was really Montana with a full deck against Marino with a half a deck. Joe got the MVP award, his second in four years, and he deserved it, passing for 331 yards, running for 59 yards and one touchdown.

The 49ers also did a heck of a job getting at Dan, sacking him four times and knocking him about.

"They threw the book at us," Dan Marino said later. "They blitzed a lot, they changed up their rushes and coverage. We had seen most of those schemes before. We just never saw them play that well."

There was so much expectation on the part of our team and our fans, but it didn't pan out. Losing the Super Bowl after the season we had put together made everyone a bit dejected. But for Dolphin fans, having Dan Marino there meant they would have a franchise player in Miami for many years to come. In 1983, he was Rookie of the Year and the first rookie ever named to the Pro Bowl. In 1984, he was voted the Most Valuable Players award. It was clear—the sky was the limit.

On December 2, 1985, the Chicago Bears thought the sky was the limit. They were 12–0 and hoping to go through the season undefeated when they came down to play us in the Orange Bowl. It was a Monday Night Game, and a hyped-up thing. The Bears had given up just a field goal in their three previous games. And everyone was kind of in awe of their "46" defense, named after one of the their former players, Doug Plank, who wore number 46. Some of the Dolphin legends were on the sidelines—Csonka, Kiick, Kuechenberg, Griese, the guys from our team that had gone 17–0 in 1972. Beating the Bears was a pride thing for everyone associated with the Miami Dolphins.

Nat Moore had two touchdown passes and caught a lot of balls and was the big player in that game. Another touchdown came when Dan threw a pass that skipped off a guy's helmet, and Mark Clayton caught the ball and went in for a touchdown. We ended up beating Chicago, 38–24, their only loss of the year. They wound up with a 15–1 record and a big season. That win gave us a 9–4 record. We finished 12–4, but were knocked out in the AFC championship game, 31–14, by New England, who hadn't beaten us in a long time. Then the Patriots went up against the Bears in the Super Bowl and were just slaughtered.

The 1986 season was an up and down year, one of the unhappiest times I ever had on the Dolphins. It was a season that Don Shula seemed testier than ever.

One of Shula's worst tirades took place that season against the whole team in one of our film sessions. The punch line was something like "I can go 8–8 with 22 guys off the street." That's quite a statement.

I looked at Dan Marino. Dan Marino looked at Bruce Hardy. Bruce Hardy looked at me. We all looked at Don Shula like did-he-say-what-I-think-he-said? We were stunned.

Special tantrums, wild rages, veiled threats—all have always been part of the Don Shula package. With players, some only needed a pat on the back, some needed to be threatened with job security, while others needed to be yelled at constantly. Whatever it took to motivate, Shula did it very well. And some he saved for the refs. He worked them over. He worked them over big-time. You never saw any of those dishes placed next to him for sound.

A lot of the stuff he pulls with refs happens during time-outs when TV is selling its razor blades or life insurance or beer. That's when the ref comes over.

This one guy had made a couple of calls Shula didn't like. He said, "Joe, Joe, come here. Goddammit, you screwed that call up."

Joe just waved him off and didn't come over. After three or four more plays, Shula was super-pissed, but his voice at first didn't show it.

"Joe, please come here. I just want to talk to you for a minute." The ref came over and Shula stopped smiling and started on him. "You asshole, you blew that damn call."

"Don, this isn't like you," the ref said calmly and turned and walked away.

Shula was constantly aware of which officials were doing a good job and those that weren't. And when he thought an official was doing a fine job, he made a point of letting him know it.

Those were the kinds of games Shula played with players and officials—psychological things.

We wound up 1986 with an 8–8 record. Talk about mediocre. The one game that kind of caught the flavor of that whole season was against the Jets on September 21, 1986. Dan Marino hit on 30 of 50 attempts for 448 yards and 6 touchdowns. Duper and Clayton both had over 100 yards receiving. Incredible performances. All that and we lost the game, 51–45, in overtime. It was a heartbreaker.

On December 22, 1986, we played our final game in

the Orange Bowl, losing to New England, 34–27. That win gave the Patriots the AFC East title. For Miami it was the end of an era, the end of 21 seasons at the Orange Bowl, a place that had always been very good for the Dolphins. Nobody on the team was too emotional about it being our last game in the Orange Bowl until we walked off the field. Then we started thinking about the old place with the breeze sometimes coming off the ocean through the open end. It felt like Miami.

Playing in the Orange Bowl the Dolphins were 110–38–3 lifetime for a .738 regular season percentage—and that's including the years in the late 1960s when the team was bad. As I have said, the home field edge is like the twelfth man on the team.

The new home of the Dolphins, Joe Robbie Stadium, was designed to accommodate baseball also in the future. Part of Don Shula's deal in the new place was a skybox reserved for his use in the right-hand corner of the stadium. That's where home plate would be for baseball. You would have thought he would have been pleased with that, but he was just the opposite.

"They gave me a box out in the corner of the stadium," he looked at me with irritation. "You can't see anything out of it. I had them move it, so that I'm behind the goalposts straight down the field, not sideways."

"But if you kept the other," I said, "you'd be able to watch eighty-one games right behind home plate when they play baseball at Joe Robbie Stadium."

But that made no difference to Shula—football was what he cared about the most.

Then there was the time that the actor Don Johnson was brought into the locker room. The guy is a big star, and everyone made a fuss about him. Some of the players even went over and asked for his autograph. Our public relations guy brought Johnson over and introduced him to Don Shula.

"Hi, Don Johnson, Miami Vice."

"Congratulations," Shula said. "You guys are doing a great job on the streets. Keep it up. We've got to keep that crime down."

It wouldn't surprise me if Shula actually thought that Don Johnson was a cop.

In 1987, the strike clouds were all over the place again. It was getting to be like a nightmare movie rerun. Only this time there were more management games played than usual. During the preseason, management told guys that were being cut from teams to sign a piece of paper that gave them a thousand dollars each but committed them to come back and play if there were replacement games. That was a deal Tex Schramm of the Dallas Cowboys cooked up. He and the other executives had learned in 1982 that no games equaled no cash. Even before the strike was announced, the owners were setting themselves up with what they called "replacement teams."

We got two games in before the strike was called on September 22. One of those games, against New England in our season opener, is a time I won't soon forget. The only thing I thought I had to worry about on that rainy Sunday in Foxboro was staying dry. But Reggie Roby injured his right leg in the first quarter—and there I was, pressed into service, backing him up. The last time I had punted in a regular game was fifteen years before, in my senior year at Virginia Tech. The only time I had punted in the National Football League was in a preseason game against New Orleans in the Superdome in 1975.

My leg was on, though, even though coming out there was a bit nerve-wracking, what with the wet weather and the ball feeling heavy and slick. Three of my punts traveled 42, 45, and 44 yards. Two of them rolled out of bounds at the New England two-yard line. I wasn't trying to do anything fancy—all I wanted to do was get the ball across the line of scrimmage.

Then, with a couple of minutes left in the game, Marino was kicked in the face by a New England player, and I was not only the backup punter, but also the backup quarterback. I had my doubts about being the backup punter because I never practiced kicking. I wasn't nervous about replacing Dan—coming in as backup quarterback was always second nature. I hit on six of seven passes. It was just questionable timekeeping that kept me from running one more play from the Patriots' eight-yard line and pulling the game out.

Reggie Roby was the Bob Kuechenberg of 1987. We had a meeting before the 1987 strike and Reggie, a real quiet type, was there seemingly going along with everything. And the next thing you know, he's crossing the line. He and Liffort Hobley, the strong safety from Louisiana State. Hobley claimed he needed the paycheck. Roby never claimed anything. Hobley and Roby were kind of nonprime-time scabs.

But around the league there were some big-time scabs: Joe Montana, Danny White, Jim Everett, and

Howie Long. Lawrence Taylor also crossed the line, but with what was going on with him and drugs back then, it must have been a confusing time in his life. J. T. Smith of the Cardinals was a scab. He caught 90-plus balls that year as a receiver, 15 in one scab game. What the hell do his stats mean aside from demeaning the records of players who accomplished things in regular competition?

There was a lot more bitterness in the 1987 strike than there was in the lockout of 1982, when there were no games played. This time around there were what they called "replacement teams" playing. They can call them replacement teams forever. I call those guys who played scabs.

Tex Schramm, who is a very good friend of Don Shula's, was supposedly the one who came up with the idea behind the replacement games. It was a desperate move prompted by the fact that in the league contract with the television networks they had to put bodies out there.

John Robinson, the Rams' coach said: "It's not like you're getting them out of a tavern somewhere. Okay, we got some out of a tavern." They got some out of a tavern, some from everywhere.

There's always talk about the integrity of the National Football League. The integrity is questionable, and that was clearly shown in the 1987 strike by the league bringing those scabs in off the street to keep things going so that games would be televised and all that money from sponsors could be generated. The whole thing was a joke, and the public realized it. The large majority of those scabs could not play football. Some of them tried to be hard-asses, but all their being there did was make the whole season a joke.

You remember my telling you how Don Shula had once told us in a clubhouse meeting that he could go 8–8 with a bunch of guys off the street. Well, the strike of 1987 sure gave him his big chance. Those scabs, a bunch of guys off the street who played for him, won one game and lost two. He would have never made 8–8.

A great trivia question came out of that strike. What were the circumstances of the first regular season win by a team in Joe Robbie Stadium? The answer—the first win was by a damn scab team. And Don Shula and Joe Robbie proudly accepted game balls from those scabs. It's like former Dolphin publicist Bob Kearney said: "Don Shula has a high threshold of pain for someone else's pain."

All around the league we walked the line, and labor organizers walked with us. The wives and children of striking players walked the line, too. There was tension and hostility all over the place. We yelled at the scabs going through the line to play; the fans yelled at us. Some of us yelled at the fans. Food trucks, milk trucks, were turned around. No union truck driver would cross that line.

A bus came to pick up the scab team at Joe Robbie Stadium and take the players to the airport to play a game in Seattle. It's only a few miles from the practice fields to the airport, but they had a hell of time getting there. The bus had to go out the back way on a dirt road to the other side of the field through an opening in the fence so they wouldn't have to drive by and see us picketing and screaming at them. Talk about leaving through the back door!

That was gentle stuff compared with what was happening in other places. In one NFL city, one guy broke out the window of a bus. Another player came riding in shooting a shotgun. There were a lot of strange and violent things all over the NFL.

In Miami, we had a tough labor organizer around a lot of the time trying to keep things in order. The guy fit the old movie tough-guy image. Striking Dolphin players pulled into the parking lot in their Porsches, Jags, BMWs. Mercedeses, what have you? The organizer wasn't too happy with that scene.

"Shit," he screamed at the guys who were jockeying their cars into the lot. "Don't any of you damn guys drive a good old-fashioned American car?"

"I do," Dan Marino said.

"I do, too," I said. "Look over there."

Side by side in the parking lot were our cars—Chevy Blazers.

"That's more like it," the organizer smiled.

We smiled back, but we didn't dare tell him that we were driving those Blazers because we both had commercial deals with Chevrolet dealers.

After four missed weeks of action all the striking players finally came back in. We went back perhaps one week too early because the quality of football being played was shit and the TV sponsors were about ready to drop out.

When we came back, there were 22 scabs that could be carried on the roster by each NFL team: 11 that could fill in on offense and 11 hanging around to play defense. That was insurance by the teams and the league—part of their plan—in case of some kind of ploy by the Players Association to walk out again.

Shula scheduled two-a-day practices at Joe Robbie Stadium for veterans only. Then we went back to work with the scabs. It was not a really happy scene.

Kyle Mackey, the former Jet quarterback and a scab for the Dolphins, came into the locker room and tried to shake hands with Dan Marino and me. We didn't even offer him the back of our hand, but we did turn our ass on him. David Shula, Don Shula's son, who was on the scene as an assistant coach, couldn't understand it. He started talking about how Mackey had played for the replacement team and was so gutsy. He played so well that the Dolphins were 1–2 when we returned after the strike. The two losses were to conference foes, which really hurt. Thanks a lot!

The locker room scene and the practice scene were strikers and scabs together. It was crowded and tense. Somehow they made room for all of us. But they couldn't do much about the tension. Dan Marino was a member of the Players Association Executive Committee and our player rep. He was so pissed off that he'd pull a curtain around his locker every day and wouldn't even look at those scabs. And a bunch of us would just sit there in what we called the executive suite, segregated from those scabs. There were no fights, but in the practices, the scabs got hit a little harder than was normal by the guys who had been out there striking.

Today if you look at the Miami Dolphin *Media Guide* there is no identification that shows in any way a bunch of scabs played in 1987. In fact they even list those guys in the all-time roster in the same way they list the regular team.

On picture day in 1987, none of the regular players on the Dolphins showed up, so they took a picture of the replacement team—the Miami Dolphins' scab team. For a while Shula had that picture of the scabs on his wall. He must have been proud of them or something. Talk about vomiting.

The strikes have caused a lot of hardships, some gains for NFL players. We all lost a lot of money in 1987. I lost almost $88,000, and I wasn't way up there in salary. What was gained? Who knows? It hasn't even been settled yet.

A kind of P.S. to the whole thing is the attitude of Everson Walls, the old Dallas cornerback who was with the Giants in 1990. After he intercepted two balls against Washington that gave him 48 for his career, he bragged a few days later: "I've got all 48 footballs at home, and I'm keeping all of them. I feel management has made enough money off the players." They sure have. Talk about balls!

The 1987 season was not only the year of a bitter strike, it was also a time my role on the Dolphins started to change. Through virtually every season I was a member of the team, my place, when I was not playing quarterback or holding for extra points or field-goal attempts, was on the sidelines right next to Don Shula. I'd be standing there, Shula's hands would be folded, and he would seem to be in perfect control but doing nothing. He scarcely ever looked at me. But he'd say: "We need a call for third down."

I'd make the call. The play would be sent in by hand

signals. The quarterback always had the option to change the play that was sent into him. If no play was sent in or signalled in from the sidelines, we would point at the quarterback and that meant he would call the play. I made so many calls through all those seasons, and the system worked very nicely. In fact, former Philly head coach Dick Vermeil said on television that Don Shula told him: "Don Strock had total control of our offense. He knows it in and out, probably as good as if not better than Bob Griese."

After David Shula joined the Miami Dolphins operation in 1984, we had a nice working relationship for a few years. I was still doing the play calling, and David would be up in the booth and I'd be conferring with him on the phone.

Coach Shula would ask: "What does Dave like? What do you like?" We weren't always that far apart, and the system still worked pretty well. I knew the system in and out, and I helped David learn it.

Then all of a sudden, in 1985, things changed dramatically. Norm Braman, the owner of the Philadelphia Eagles, said: "Well, you know he is a Shula and it runs in the family." David Shula had supposedly just been offered the head coach job in Philadelphia after the Chicago Bears game. I never understood that. Does coaching success run in the family?

David Shula was very young at that time—he worked very hard, studied hard. He learned the offensive system inside-out. He made himself into a good football coach, but at that point in his career he might have been too young to take over the responsibilities of an NFL franchise, but that's the kind of thing we'll never know.

In a preseason game in August of 1987—the first game ever played in Joe Robbie Stadium—Dan Marino dislocated the ring finger on his throwing hand. Dolphin management came to the conclusion that they needed another body at the quarterback position, just in case. So Ron Jaworski, released by the Philadelphia Eagles, was signed by Miami off the waiver wire.

But the coming to Miami of Ron Jaworski was accompanied by hype and big fanfare. They even held up a practice a couple of hours so he could make it. I thought that was foolish bullshit. He was the kind of guy who couldn't and didn't add anything to the Miami Dolphins.

That first year he was signed for basically the same salary I was making. But for 1988, Ron Jaworski was signed for the second year of a two-year deal for $425,000 something. I was making $350,000. They offered me $385,000. That pissed me off, and I told them, "I'm not going to take a penny less than this guy. He has never done a damn thing for the Dolphins and probably never will."

I thought after the service I had given the Dolphins for all those years I should be making more than a guy they picked off the waiver list. The whole thing was disheartening. Shula didn't stick up for me. For me it got down to a pride and principle thing. The guys on the team said, "Just sign and come in."

But I said, "I'm not made that way."

I had three options. One was to sign and bury my pride. Option number two was to be traded or cut. The third option was the one I chose—sitting out and making them withdraw their contract. That would give them no compensation for me. Shula was quoted in the *Dolphin Digest*: "The feeling of management was that since the two sides weren't able to get together, Strock should be given an opportunity to shop his services. The backup quarterback job now comes down to those we have in camp. It will seem a little strange without Don on the sidelines."

I sat it out, spending my time during the preseason of 1988 being a sports host at the Doral Park Silver Golf Course. I kept in shape and worked out every day with Mark Duper, who was also holding out.

That was a strange and stormy time. The sports pages in Miami were filled with all kinds of stories about friction between me and David Shula. There were reports that I didn't have any arm strength left, that I couldn't do this, couldn't do that. And I kept getting those damn phone calls from reporters. I'm generally a pretty calm guy, but all of that hornet's nest got to me. Somebody was trying to make himself look good at my expense and over my reputation. I was always a team guy with a lot of loyalty to the Dolphin organization. Now I was totally alienated.

After Miami lost their first game of the 1988 season (on its way to a 6–10 record), I called Don Shula. I told him that I would appreciate it if he could get all those people to stop calling me about the Dolphins and him and David. I told him that I had no comment and didn't want to comment. And he said doing that was just as if I were saying bad things.

I was shocked by that statement. After so many years of loyal service I still can't believe that's how it all ended. I knew then that the relationship between the Miami Dolphins and Don Strock was over.

That was it. That was the last time I spoke to Don Shula in my role as player and in his role as a coach. I was a little surprised at the way it happened. Maybe I shouldn't have been.

I thought about how other guys, marquee players on the Dolphins, had been chewed up by the system. Larry Csonka holding out and then getting out. All-Pro Ed Newman asking for a raise after being hurt one season and also getting left out in the cold. A. J. Duhe released after injuries. Bob Baumhower released after injuries...

Pro football is a business. In the back of my mind, I guess I never thought my time with the Miami Dolphins would end the way it did.

But there was more to my ending with the Miami Dolphins than a contract and dollars and cents. It was all about something you couldn't put a price on.

It was about pride and principle, my own self-worth!

BROWNS/COLTS

THE first time I spoke to Art Modell, the owner of the Cleveland Browns, was after the second week of the 1988 season. Bernie Kosar, their starting quarterback, had injured his elbow in their season opener. In the Browns' second game, against the Jets, Cleveland's second-string quarterback, Gary Danielson, broke his ankle. All they had left was Mike Pagel. They needed a quarterback, and as Art Modell said, they didn't know if I would be interested, but I was their "number one choice to fill the hole at quarterback."

At 9:30 P.M. on a Tuesday evening I listened to my answering machine. There were three messages in a row from Ernie Accorsi, the Browns' football operations director. They all said to call him if I was interested in joining the Browns. The fourth message was from my agent Jerry Kapstein: "Don't call anyone," it said. "Don't call anyone until you speak to me." Talk about the wonders of answering machines.

What happened after that was a conference call that was more like a board meeting.

"Mr. Kapstein, this is Art Modell."

"Mr. Strock, this is Ernie Accorsi."

"Mr. Modell, hello, this is Jerry Kapstein."

Then my wife Debby got on the line.

"Is that your secretary, Mr. Strock?" Modell asked.

"No, sir, that's my wife."

"How do you do, Mrs. Strock? This is Mr. Modell."

We finally got it all squared away around 12:30 A.M. That was about three hours on the phone. I agreed on a prorated contract for $480,000 plus a $5,000 bonus per start. I made more in Cleveland than I had asked for in Miami, and the Dolphins got no compensation for my being signed. I was 37 years old and on my way to the Cleveland Browns.

Cleveland is one of the great sports towns. And Municipal Stadium is a great place for pro football. Grass, snow, wind, rain, overcast, and outside in the north. Outside in the north is very hard to find anymore. They have the greatest fans. More than 80,000 come out hours before game time. Then when the game is over, a lot of them drive down to the Flats, a renovated area of the city, and have some beers and food and talk about what happened. Then they go to Richfield that night, a forty-minute drive, to watch the Cleveland Cavs play NBA basketball.

The one guy I knew pretty well on Cleveland was Bernie Kosar from his days playing quarterback for the University of Miami. We had played together in several golf tournaments in Florida. It was after Gary Danielson got hurt that Bernie said: "Just call Don Strock. He's the guy we need."

The Cleveland coach, Marty Schottenheimer, was a

players' coach. He had played football up until the late 1960s himself. He was about 45. He's from the coal regions around McDonald, Pennsylvania, where he grew up tough. A former linebacker, a special teams player, Marty came up through the coaching ranks as a special teams coach and an assistant defensive coach. He liked the physical part of the game, and I and the other guys enjoyed playing for him and played hard every minute. Players like Kevin Mack, a real bull of a guy, and Ernest Byner, called E.B., an amazing talent who never quits, kind of typified the Browns in 1988.

The team had that tough work ethic, but every day we were treated to fine food from a different restaurant or pizzeria. They'd bring batches of good things to eat into the locker room at camp at Baldwin-Wallace College in Berea, Ohio.

I was with the Browns only three days when I found myself standing with Bernie Kosar on the sidelines for a Monday Night Game against the Indianapolis Colts. I was in street clothes; Bernie was in street clothes.

Marty Schottenheimer had told the media: "We signed Don Strock because he's experienced, because he has played in big games, because he's intelligent, and he was the best quarterback available, in our minds. One of the reasons we like him is because of his intelligence. So we don't expect him to have a difficult time picking up our system—even though ours is nothing like the Dolphins'."

It *was* nothing like the Dolphins', and it was tough learning the Cleveland system. I had some of the plays written out on a wristband (the coach's secretary made a new wristband for me each week) because I hadn't memorized everything the Browns did. And, fortunately, I had the wristband when three weeks later I played against Seattle in Cleveland when Mike Pagel dislocated his shoulder on a blocked field-goal attempt. Then in what was my first start in five years, I went up against Philadelphia, and we beat them, 19–3. That was something special, with my family and friends watching back home on local TV, seeing me play for the Browns wearing number 12.

Several weeks later, December 12, 1988, it was down to Miami—Monday Night Football, the Browns against the Dolphins and Kosar against Marino. Bernie's elbow had come around.

Don Shula was quoted in the newspapers: "It will be different seeing Strock on the other side of the field. But it's been quite a while since he's been here. I'm sure he's aware of our signals, so we'll all have to take some precautions. All you do is give a couple false ones. That'll create doubt as to whether to regard the actual signals. We're more concerned about Kosar."

I got a bit of a charge seeing fans in the stands wearing number 12 Don Strock jerseys for the Browns and others wearing number 10 Don Strock jerseys for the Dolphins. The signs: "Strock, we miss you," and "Don, we love you," made me feel good. But I didn't expect any action in that game and didn't even warm up.

The Dolphins had a 5–9 record. The Browns were 9–5. But going into the game, having been in this situation before with the Dolphins, I knew how dangerous Miami could be in a Monday Night Game at home, even though Cleveland had the better record.

I was rooting for Cleveland, yet inside of me I was also rooting for my friends on the Dolphins as I watched the game play out from the sidelines. I got a charge seeing Dan Marino throw the 193rd touchdown pass of his career to break Bob Griese's Miami career record. Then I got a scare seeing John Offerdahl ram into Bernie Kosar with eight minutes left in the fourth quarter. Fortunately, Bernie left the field under his own power.

With Bernie hurting and Mike Pagel and Gary Danielson on injured reserve, I was the only one left on Cleveland available to play quarterback. I came in with the Dolphins leading 31–17. The reception I got was something I'll never forget—a two-minute standing ovation! I'm sure Don Shula was not real happy about that, but most of the Dolphins on the sidelines were rooting for me.

You don't know what it's like unless you've been there, but the feeling for me was weird. On the field in Miami wearing the uniform of the Cleveland Browns and competing against the team I had played with for fifteen years and against Dan Marino, one of my best friends in the whole world. I thought of how many times I had played against that defense on the practice field. It was a backup's dream come true.

I audibled to Ozzie Newsome and dumped the ball over the middle to him for a big gain. That was a play that used to be popular—I guess some people must have thought only a fifteen-year veteran and an eleven-year veteran could remember it. Then I threw a touchdown pass to Reggie Langhorne, and we were down by just seven. The Dolphins came back onto the field, and

Dan Marino threw an interception. We got the ball back. I threw a touchdown pass to Reggie Langhorne and we were tied, 31-all with something like fifty-nine seconds to go in the game.

But it was good news–bad news. Fifty-nine seconds for Dan Marino is eternity. He hit a couple of key passes, and they scored a touchdown in about twenty-five seconds, taking the lead again.

With just a few seconds left in the game and down 38–31 we were about fifty yards from the end zone. We ran a play and then I called a time-out. Everybody thought the game was over. Shula starting walking off the field.

"We have one more play!" I told him.

He gives me a look like "What's going on?"

And I said, "We have one more damn play!!"

I'm glad I did it, what with Ron Jaworski and Dan Marino and others coming over to me to shake my hand. It made them all walk back off the field. Then I threw a Hail Mary which naturally didn't hit, and that was it.

As I was walking off the field, there wasn't a guy on the Dolphin side who didn't come over to slap me or shake my hand. I went through the tunnel and waited for Shula to come off the field. He walked right toward me. I don't know what he was thinking, but he never stopped.

It was a great homecoming for me after all the turmoil of my ending with the Dolphins. As I said, I didn't expect to play and didn't know what the reaction would be if I did play.

Later, watching the tape of the game, it was so

surprising to see how the announcers, Dan Dierdorff, Frank Gifford, and Al Michaels downplayed the whole thing. It was puzzling because they seemed to miss the boat on what was a good story—the fact that I was returning to Miami after fifteen years as a player there. The standing ovation was shown but no mention was made as to its significance. A lot of people called me up later and said: "Don, they acted like you were a stranger, never been in Miami before, a brand new guy."

Nobody knows what happened in the ABC Monday Night Football production meeting. But all I know is that they had a great story line and they made believe they knew nothing about it.

Chris Berman, of ESPN, said afterward: "The whole coverage was unbelievable, Walter Mitty revisited. It gave me chills."

Cleveland's Municipal Stadium is one of the greatest places for a football game in the world. The fans there give the Browns solid support and every game is a sellout. There is always a constant noise—either a hum or outright cheering for the Browns. Even during television time-outs there is always something going on. When the opposing team is operating, the din can split your eardrum, but when the Browns run their plays there's much more quiet.

The "dog pound" or bullpen is a section that backs onto Lake Erie. It's the only open space in the stadium. What it is is really just a bleacher. At one time those used to be the cheapest seats in the stadium. Now people trade in great seats at the 45-yard line to get a place in the "dog pound," because they want to be closer to the action. "The Dawgs," the Cleveland defensive backs, go down and start slapping high fives with those fans there, and the scene is always riotous. The fans wear masks with dog bones on them, and that makes for some strange sight. But even stranger is all the stuff those people throw—golf balls, eggs, snowballs, soda cans, whatever they can get some distance on.

I was in Municipal Stadium for a game against Houston the last week of the 1988 season, a week before Christmas. Heavy snow was falling. The field was frozen, rock hard, and painted green for television. Guys were running around with brooms sweeping snow off the yard lines. And there I was filling in again for Bernie Kosar, who watched the whole thing from the sidelines wearing his rally cap.

I was wearing rubber-bottomed, flat shoes with no spikes. And with my deep tan, I guess you could say I was kind of an oddity playing there while the wind was howling off Lake Erie and the snow was swirling. It was cold.

That was football—an old stadium on a beautiful day. Nobody left that jam-packed place. There were signs like "All I want for Christmas is a play-off berth." And "Houston—repent the end is near!" And "Shades of George Blanda."

I didn't look like or feel much like George Blanda as the game got under way. The Oilers intercepted me each of the first three series. One of them was returned by Houston safety Domingo Bryant for 36 yards and a touchdown. I was four for six passing, but three of my passes were to them. Things just were not going our way.

But if I was having my troubles, there was a cameraman out there on the field whom I felt even sorrier for. The ground crew had pushed all the snow into a pile in the back of the end zone. One of our defensive backs was covering a guy from Houston. They bumped. The Oiler player plowed into that cameraman and just buried him into the snow, knocking him unconscious. The "dog pound" people showed no mercy. They threw snowballs, golf balls, and unmentionables at the guy who was down and out. It was pretty wild. The game had to be stopped for five or ten minutes before some order was restored.

I restored some order in the second half—looking a lot at the plastic band I had taped onto my wrist where the game plan was. They'd say, "Number 50," and I'd just look at that band and run it. Everything came together, and I moved the Browns downfield on touchdown drives of 63 yards, 78 yards, 89 yards.

With 6:23 left, I drilled my second touchdown pass, this one for 22 yards to Webster Slaughter. That gave us a 28–23 win and put Cleveland into the play-offs as a wild-card team.

I wound up "Player of the Game," passing 25 of 41 for 326 yards. I remember those numbers. How could I forget them! Marty Schottenheimer told me after the game that was the most yardage any Cleveland team ever threw against Houston.

The team was lit up, especially tight end Ozzie Newsome. "This is some story," he said. "Look at that Don Strock—a guy who spent the first four or five weeks of the season on the golf course. And he won it for us." Marty Schottenheimer also got a good line in. "Don's got some zip on the ball. Maybe it's because he hasn't had to throw it much the past fifteen years." Marty was kidding, of course, because he knew that I spent fifteen years practicing, and you throw more in practice than you do in games.

The one who seemed most impressed with my performance was Art Modell, a hands-on owner, who was at practice every day. He called down from his box to the locker room to congratulate me. "Don Strock," he said afterward, "is the most unflappable quarterback I've ever seen, and that includes Bernie Kosar."

Unfortunately, we got beat in the wild-card game, and the season was over for the Browns. Right after the game, Marty said he wanted to talk to me. We sat down in his office. "Don, we appreciate all you've done for the Browns, and we want you to come back next year."

"I'd like to," I told him. "This was the most enjoyable season I ever had in the NFL."

You know how life is and how things work. Well, a few days later I was driving in my car, and a bulletin came over the radio that Marty had resigned as coach of the Browns. I was a bit stunned.

In 1989, I had expected to be back on the Cleveland Browns, on the same team with Eric Metcalf, but that connection never came to be. His father, Terry Metcalf, and I came out the same year and played against each other in the 1973 Coaches' All America Football Game in Lubbock, Texas, the last time they ever had that game. It would have been interesting being with Eric Metcalf,

Terry's son. Some say that kind of thing dates you. I say that's a sign of longevity.

I wound up in midseason of 1989 as a member of the Indianapolis Colts, a team in need of some backup help at quarterback.

The first person I saw when I arrived was Ron Meyer, the coach. He was in the whirlpool.

"First of all, Strock, stay away from my secretaries—that Florida tan will get you in trouble."

I smiled. Then he gave me a look and said, "What the hell are you doing still playing this game at your age?"

"I feel I can still play?"

"So do we. That's why you're here."

The Indianapolis setup is super high tech compared with the Dolphins and Browns. Their state-of-the-art complex is excellent, with a whirlpool that seats thirty, a sauna for twenty people, a huge steam room, two racquetball courts, thirty offices at least, an artificial turf field and two grass fields. I knew there was a lot of talent there. I thought it was a Super Bowl caliber team.

I never knew much about Eric Dickerson, the person. I had just watched him play and knew that when he was acquired from the Rams in 1987 it meant instant identity for Indianapolis. With all the yards he's gained and with him being the franchise, I always thought that, like Marino in Miami and Kosar in Cleveland, he'd be the team leader. Well, how wrong can a guy be.

The guy that was right about him was Tony Kornheiser, writing in the *Washington Post:* "Dickerson's sense of commitment is like a parking meter. It's fine as long as you feed it money every twelve minutes."

The second week I was with the Colts, we had a team meeting after the Miami game, a game Dickerson didn't play in at all, claiming he was nursing a bad hamstring.

He got up to speak—and it was disgusting to sit there and listen. As I remember it, this is what he said. "I'm a superstar," he said. "I'm a stud. I like to be on talk shows. I know I'm headed to the Hall of Fame...but I can't put up with people on this team who are just here to collect a paycheck or who are content to be mediocre."

I had never heard words like that from any other player to his teammates in all my seventeen years in the league. And I'd been around all kinds of players. But that was just Dickerson warming up.

He continued lashing out at his teammates, telling them how they didn't want to win, and how they seemed content to be 7-9 or 8-8 in the won-lost record.

"You play like you practice," he snapped. That was some statement coming from him. He didn't do anything in practice so that you would notice.

"I have this year and I have next year on my contract," Dickerson continued. "I'll be willing to be here for the rest of my career for the same amount of money I'm making right now if we can only get to the big game—the Super Bowl."

I was sitting there thinking, of course you will, you're making a million eight, or whatever.

After the team meeting finally broke up and we got out of there, one of our coaches said: "Now I know why the Rams traded him—they're probably still laughing about it."

The Rams got so much for him—five number ones, three twos, etc., etc. Talk about tearing the guts out of a team!

Eric Dickerson is a presence with that number 29 on his jersey and the goggles, the whole nine yards. He's a talent. Maybe the best runner that has ever played the game. But he can't block and he can't catch. He just wants the ball twenty-five or thirty times a game.

As the season moved on, I'd see him go over to a receiver on the Colts. "How many did you get today?"

The guy would answer: "I got 109."

And Dickerson would smile: "I got 137."

Guys like Dickerson seem to me to be more concerned about yards they get, their own image, not whether they win or lose. And that kind of stuff gets contagious and infects the other guys on the team, too.

Dickerson came out in the paper saying that playing behind the Indianapolis offensive line was like playing Russian roulette, that playing behind them was like waiting for the bullet to go off. He added that a running back commits suicide behind those guys. The offensive line didn't take kindly to that. Management certainly didn't. Coach Ron Meyer had Dickerson in his office several times, telling him that football is a team game and that his attitude was not really helpful. But nothing stopped Eric. I didn't talk to him at all except for hello; he was very standoffish.

"Everyone has this obsession that my teammates and I don't get along," Dickerson has said. "There are maybe three or four guys here I don't see eye to eye with, but it's a squad of forty-five. There are guys I don't care for and they don't care for me. But on Sundays I'm going to play hard for them. When the game is over, they're not going to come to my house and

I'm not going to come to their house. On the field we're teammates. Off the field, we're nothing."

In 1990, Dickerson missed eighty days with the Colts, holding out for a contract extension, which he got—four years worth more than $11 million. The fans in Indianapolis booed the hell out of him when he returned to play for the Colts. "No big deal," he said. "I don't get caught up in that."

Eric Dickerson is definitely not a house favorite in Indianapolis—with the fans or with the players. His nickname is Dick. I think that's quite appropriate.

Colt quarterback Jack Trudeau out of Illinois is a tough guy, one who has taken a lot of hits he shouldn't have taken, but he took them. Jack is one of the guys I've met along the way with the weirdest eating tastes. He can't eat anything mixed, nothing with cheese on it, no pizza. He'll eat steaks and baked potatoes but nothing on it, salad no dressing. He's very opinionated about food and lots of things. And he is definitely not an Eric Dickerson fan. He told me to make sure to put that in the book. So, Jack, there it is.

I was with the Colts for three weeks when Jack was injured. Tom Ramsey was behind him in the team's depth chart as quarterback. But I got a call from one of the coaches: "You're probably going to start this week against Buffalo."

I said, "Okay." What could I say? But I was concerned. I knew the system, but not all of it. And I had never even taken any offensive snaps. My main concern was the morale in the locker room. How can a guy just take over and play when guys have been there for years? What about Tom Ramsey? Over a couple of beers, I told

Tom what was going down. Tom took the news okay; it seemed he was used to the whole system there being in disarray. As it turned out I didn't start, so all of the talking was stirring up problems where there didn't have to be any.

That was one instance that showed the trouble with the Indianapolis franchise. Being there wasn't nearly as positive an experience as being with Cleveland, because the Colts are a franchise with a lot of problems. It was like the old expression that winners find a way to win and losers somehow find a way to lose. In Indianapolis, you always had the feeling they were waiting for something bad to happen. In Cleveland, they were always trying to make something good happen.

Ron Meyer was one of the bright spots at Indianapolis. He showed me the difference between a coaches' coach and a players' coach. I always think of his great line: After a tough loss, he said, "You know what the best part of this is? We get to do it again next Sunday." Ron also showed a lot of consideration for the players. He stopped the team from doing our running outdoors the last six weeks of the season because it was too cold. We met at the compound and then drove in our own cars to practice indoors at the Hoosier Dome.

The one who basically runs the team is Jim Irsay, the general manager. He played for Ron Meyer at SMU with Eric Dickerson and Craig James. When the Historic Landmarks Commission of Indiana asked Jim Irsay to compose a letter for a time capsule that will be opened in 2090, Irsay wrote: "Believe me, [Dickerson] was something to see on Sunday afternoons at the Hoosier Dome. He was the greatest runner the game has ever seen." So you can see how things evolved at Indianapolis and where Irsay's train of thought is.

It was Jim Irsay's father, Bob Irsay, the owner, who moved the franchise to Indianapolis from Baltimore. For a lot of people that move caused some unhappy feelings. "I think he's crazy," was what Ray Perkins, who had been a receiver for the Baltimore Colts, said. "If they're going to take the Colts out of Baltimore, there should be no more Colts. Call them the Indianapolis Air Conditioners. That's how Irsay made his money."

No one needed air conditioners one day during Christmas week when Bob Irsay arranged for a lavish party, and all the guys on the team had to make an appearance. It took us quite some time to drive to his big ranch in Carmel, Indiana. It was very, very cold. The wind-chill had to be minus 45 degrees, and the roads were slick. The party was inside a big barn, and it was a beautiful setup.

Guys on the team spread the word that the only people you had to make sure you saw were Coach Ron Meyer and his wife and Bob Irsay and his wife.

I spotted the Irsays. "Mr. Irsay, Don Strock, nice to meet you."

"Don," he smiled. "Nice to see you here. What are you doing now?"

His wife cut in. "Honey, he plays for us now."

"Oh, that's right."

I could never tell whether he was serious or what. But he was the one back in 1983 who sent John Elway to the Denver Broncos with the parting shot: "He'll never be any good."

Going into our final regular season game on December 24 we were 8–7. We were going down to play New Orleans, knowing that if we won we were in the play-offs. We got beat 41 to something, and that ended our season.

After the game, I was walking through the tunnel as Bob Irsay and his wife and their entourage were walking out. They saw me. "Don," Irsay said. "Maybe next year you'll know the offense and we'll get you in there to play."

"Yeah, sure, thanks a lot," I said.

The flight back to Indianapolis, for me, was kind of symbolic because I was a man without a place to go. You see, on December 22, on a night when the temperature was minus 20-something and minus 50-something in wind-chill, the condo that I rented in Indianapolis had burned down. I guess somebody was giving me a sign that it might be a good idea for me to conclude my active playing career in the National Football League.

THE CAINE BROTHERS, STEROIDS, AND OTHER GOODIES

THE National Football League makes a big deal today about drug testing, steroids, substance abuse. But that stuff is all part of the game, always will be, and, as long as it's around, it's going to be controversial. Chip Oliver, the Raiders linebacker back in the 1970s, said: "If Pete Rozelle, the commissioner, put a lock on the pill bottle, half the players would fall asleep in the third quarter."

I don't know if it was as bad as all that, but when I first came into the league, there were many players who had their private pill boxes and bottles, their own exclusive medicine cabinet supply of stuff. And there was also the public supply of goodies.

Now, you've got to understand that not all these drugs were banned by the NFL at the time they were being used. Some, like steroids and cocaine, certainly are, but the Caine brothers, Ritalin, and other drugs the team doctors inject were not banned at the time. What's controversial is how they were used and what they did to the players in the long run. I have some strong feelings about that.

One of the major goodies that was dispersed was

Ritalin. I took it, but not regularly. About half the guys on the Dolphin roster occasionally used Ritalin. The team doctors would give it out in pill form. The stuff gave you a tremendous lift, a surge of energy. You'd go out onto the field and the juices were churning and you were flying.

But after the Ritalin wore off, there were some bad aftereffects. Some guys couldn't open their mouth. Talk about lockjaw. I remember one of our stars trying to drink a beer and having trouble getting his lips apart. He poured that beer all over his face.

Ritalin lasted a few years and was replaced by a type of caffeine pill to get the adrenalin going. You'd take a nap and come to the stadium late in the afternoon before a game: "Hey, doc, give me a one and one." That's what we called it, and that's what we got.

The pressure was always there—peer pressure, self-pressure, coach pressure—for guys to compete. Somehow a player always had to get himself ready to play. There was no place for thinking about what it might mean for him down the line.

One week I was so banged up that it was all I could do to spend most of my time soaking in the tub.

"You'll be able to play Sunday, won't you?" I didn't know when Shula said that if he was asking me or telling me.

"I don't know," I told him. "I'll do what's necessary when the time comes. But I'm not ready for it just now. Let's just wait until Friday."

For some it was not a question of waiting. They took what they had to when they had to.

Xylocaine—first to numb.

Novocaine—to deaden.

The Caine Brothers...

Dan Pastorini's full name is Dante Anthony Pastorini—and he was a character. Back in 1978 he helped lead the Houston Oilers into the play-offs for the first time in a long time. The Miami Dolphins were Houston's first opposition. Just before the play-offs began, he treated about twenty guys—his entire offensive unit and the supporting troops—to a big dinner. A lot of wine was consumed, and reports were that the lion's share of the stuff was imbibed by Dan.

Shortly afterward, he prepared to do battle against the Miami Dolphins. You could say he wasn't in the best of condition, what with a brace on his knee, three cracked ribs, a puffy elbow, a sensitive ankle. But Dan also had a protective cushion—the flak jacket. That was a new thing in 1978—a getup created out of the same material they use for bulletproof vests.

In the first half of that wild-card game played at the Orange Bowl the day before Christmas, Pastorini threw the ball for 261 yards, a Houston team record. He hit 20 out of 29 passes. He was something special that day. We got beat 17–9.

The flak jacket got a lot of publicity and so did Dan. But it wasn't until a few years later that he came out and admitted that part of the reason for his success, given all his physical problems, was the fact that he took two dozen shots of novocaine—a dozen to start the game and another dozen to start the second half. I guess they did the job.

There have always been guys like Dan Pastorini with a high threshold for pain and others with a low threshold for pain, and still others with just plain pain. And all of them in one way or another have wound up at the business end of a needle getting their Caine Brothers.

Dan Johnson, who was a tight end on Miami from 1983 to 1987, got shot up eleven weeks in a row in his big toe joint. He had turf toe. The toe was purple not black. Somehow, Dan played every game.

Rusty Chambers, a roommate of mine who was killed in a car crash, dislocated his pinky on the field in a tough play in a game at the Superdome in New Orleans. He came to the sidelines in a lot of pain. His finger was sticking sideways. The team doctor told everybody to crowd around Rusty to block out the view so the fans wouldn't be upset seeing Rusty get a shot. Then the doc took out a needle and shot Rusty up right in the gap between his fingers. Pulling the finger straight, the doctor taped it, and sent Rusty back out onto the playing field. Rusty didn't miss a play. The needle? Oh, the doctor slipped it under the carpet in the Dome and that damn thing might still be there rusting away.

The Caine Brothers and the Blackwood Brothers always had a lot to do with each other. Glen Blackwood had his shoulder separated. They'd grab hold of his shoulder, pull it out a little, shoot him right in the joint. Ten weeks in a row they did that, and Glen played with a separated shoulder.

His brother Lyle broke his nose while playing in a game and came back to the sidelines. They put a tongue depressor in each nostril, straightened the nose out, and shot him right between the eyes with the Caine Brothers. Then they taped Lyle up and sent him right back in. He missed just three plays the whole game.

Jon Giesler was a big left tackle who played for many years for the Dolphins. A number one draft pick out of the University of Michigan, Jon got his knee banged up pretty bad in a game. For more than ten weeks in a row he was shot in that knee three or four times before each game. It was painful. I used to wince just watching him go through it. When they finished shooting Jon up, they taped him and braced him. And then out he'd go— playing football.

After the game was over, Jon would come back into the locker room, strip down. The knee would be a sight—all swollen again. He'd be there patiently waiting for them to drain it. Then on crutches and in a lot of pain, he'd leave the stadium. All week Jon would be hobbling about on those crutches, unable to practice at all. And the sight of that huge and powerful man hobbled in pain was something you don't forget. But Jon endured to play the game he loved. Then in 1990, it all came to an end when the Miami Dolphins informed Jon Giesler that they were not renewing his contract.

Wayne Moore, out of Lamar, who played a lot of effective tackle for the Dolphins in the 1970s, went through much suffering because of a bad knee. You could definitely say that Wayne and the Caine Brothers were on very intimate terms. Weekly they drained blood and fluid and crap out of Wayne's bad knee. And every week Wayne played football. A couple of years ago,

Wayne Moore died of a heart attack. He was 44 years old.

You're a quarterback. You make a living with your arm. The doctor examines you. "You have two separated cartilages in your ribs on the right side."

"But, doctor," you say, "I throw with my right arm."

"We can take care of that," he says. "We'll inject you up and you'll be fine for about four hours."

You are fine, and after the four hours pass, you go for a couple of drinks and dinner. That's fun. But then you can't get off the barstool or the dining room chair to get home. You're frozen. You live that way for days. That was what it was like for me—like a nightmare.

In 1989, the Pittsburgh Steelers played the Miami Dolphins in a rainstorm. Dan Marino got body-slammed by a defensive back and was taken back to the locker room. The game was close.

"You've got a bruised shoulder, no separation," the doctor told him. "It won't hurt 'us' to inject your shoulder."

So Dan was shot in the right shoulder joint with the Caine Brothers. Then he came out for the second half and told Shula, "I'm ready to play."

But Shula told him that, since the team was now down by twenty points, there was no need for him to play. "I just went in there and got my shoulder shot up and you tell me that I'm not going to play? Shit!"

Now you tell me that what they did to Dan was worth it. But that's the game. That is the game.

Always joking, one of the freest spirits that I've ever seen, Jake Scott played his heart out at safety for the Dolphins from 1970 to 1975. He was bald, wore glasses and was kind of a crazy-looking guy. Jake wore number 13 and was his own man. He had played at the University of Georgia and left early to play in the Canadian Football League as a wide receiver and defensive back. Then he came back to Miami. Not a real big guy, only about 180 pounds, Jake used to love to throw his body into real big guys. It was amazing, and everyone wondered how he didn't crumble. But he had everything broken—separated shoulder, banged-up legs, etc. Jake played hurt so many times; he played in a Super Bowl with two broken wrists against the Redskins and was the MVP.

Once he had a separated shoulder and refused to take a shot to kill the pain. "If you touch me," he told the doctor, "I'm going to sue you." The doctor didn't touch him, but Jake was suspended. But he didn't back down. The whole deal was over his playing in a preseason game. Jake was an All-Pro starter, and he didn't want to take a shot for a preseason game. He didn't feel he really had to show anybody that he could still play the game. He was just a defiant type of guy.

Pain and suffering has always been a part of the game. And some players just make ghoulish jokes about it. What else can they do? Tim Foley, a Miami defensive back, always claimed that his most cherished NFL memory was "Waking up from all of my operations." A. J. Duhe, the Dolphin linebacker back in 1985, went through five operations in five months. "The next time I see a doctor," he said, "it better be for an autopsy."

Joe Rose was in the hospital scheduled to have shoulder surgery. The team physicians had recommended that he go through with it. He checked into the hospital, and they went right to work on Joe—shaving his chest, painting it, the whole nine yards. Prep! That's what they call it. Joe was prepped and ready for bright and early morning surgery. But somewhere around 5:30 in the morning he decided he wasn't going to have any part of it. So he just walked out of the hospital. Afterward he continued with his life and career, playing for the Dolphins and playing well. The question is—was the surgery needed?

Fortunately, the knife and my body didn't come into contact with each other too often. But there was the time I was scheduled to have surgery performed on my right ankle. I didn't look forward to it, but I knew I had to get it out of the way. When I entered the hospital, I was ready. They were very reassuring, giving me lines like all was in readiness, piece of cake, nothing to worry about. But with what I knew about guys getting screwed up going under the knife, I figured it wouldn't be going against my own best interests to sneak a peek at the sheet they had made out for me. I'm glad I peeked. Some moron who didn't know his left from his right had written down that the surgery was to be performed on my left ankle. Curiosity may have killed the cat, but my curiosity saved me from having them operate on my good ankle.

Steroids are a whole other ball game. The headlines have been full of that stuff. Notre Dame coach Lou Holtz denied he approved of steroids. Steve Corsen did steroids forever. They checked his heart rate while he was sleeping and found that it was 160. And now he needs a new heart. Hopefully they'll find one in time.

Brian Sochia, the nose tackle on the Dolphins, was suspended for three games at the start of the 1990 season, after they suddenly discovered that he was using steroids. He was a pumped-up guy who was on steroids for three, four years. Sochia was finally caught when he failed a substance abuse test because of steroids in his system.

The Good Lord said your body can hold only so much, be that big, get that strong. Steroid use creates freaks of nature. Why do guys go for it? To get bigger. To get stronger to compete. Again, it's self-pressure, peer pressure, but pressure from the coaches that makes players put that stuff into their system with pills, liquids, injections, anyway they can find to do it. But they were never actually forced to do it.

Now there's an institutionalized testing program for steroids, and the league makes a big deal of the fail-safe checks. Guys make a lot of jokes about it. For some it has its good points, in that you don't have to do any advance studying to take it. All you have to do is be ready to piss. Talk about guys being pissed off.

One year at Miami guys went into the toilet, peed into a cup and brought out the piss cup. But some guys never peed. They simply came out with a cup of "clean" piss that they had smuggled into the toilet. That led to the Jay Leno joke about the guy who was arrested for selling "clean urine" to pass drug tests. His defense was, "Hey, I just sell the stuff. I don't know what the people do with it once they get it."

The next year the word came down from on high that there would be no more smuggled "clean urine." Now the marching orders called for weenie watchers or what some called the pee patrol. That was a great idea, but how many numbers of how many cups can be mixed up when the samples are numbered: 1185635304 6340303746453733????

This next story should catch your attention. In 1987, I reported late to the Dolphins for preseason training camp. I went in to take my physical but never took a urine test or any kind of test for drugs.

I never gave it a second thought at the time. It wasn't until the next year in Cleveland that I realized how long it had been since I was tested. In 1988, when I played at Cleveland, the powers that be there just assumed that I'd already taken a urine test and didn't administer one to me until November 28, a day after my birthday. That made it a year and a half that I was in the NFL without ever being tested for drugs. So you can see no matter the fancy press releases, the drug testing program is not fail-safe by any means. I'm living proof of that fact!

The whole situation with drugs, steroids, pain-killers is bogus to my way of thinking. You must take a piss test for drugs. You pee for steroid checkups. But if they need you to play the game, they'll fix you up with anything they can. And I mean anything!

I had a lump in the back of my ear. The doctor took a look at it and apologized to me that he didn't have any kind of anesthesia handy. "Take this ice-cold can of Diet Pepsi and go back to my room," he said. "Stick the can on your ear. I'll be back in a few minutes."

Talk about primitive stuff. The cold can on the ear got it numb. The doctor came back and stuck a big needle in my ear and sucked all the crap out. Then he gave me a shot and that was the end of that.

The whole drug scene in the NFL not only turns me off but makes me cynical. Lawrence Taylor has been caught with drugs; one more time and he's supposedly banned forever from the NFL. C'mon, is that ever going to happen with a draw and a talent like him? Tony Collins, suspended forever from the league, they said. Then reinstated. Signed by the Dolphins—a three-time loser recycled. Brave New World? Bending the rules?

The classic example of a player screwed up by drugs is Hollywood Henderson. Don Shula signed Hollywood for a hundred-some thousand dollars, thinking he would show the NFL that he could rehab Henderson and turn his career around. In his book, Hollywood admitted being wired on cocaine when he talked with Shula about trying out for the Dolphins. Part of his deal with Miami was that Hollywood was obliged to go to Narc Anonymous twice a week.

Even in his good days with the Dallas Cowboys, Hollywood was never a really disciplined player because he freelanced, doing his own thing, a lot and got beat a lot. But he was an exceptional talent.

Our defensive coordinator, Bill Arnsparger, loved Hollywood's raw talent, but that was where it ended. In practice, Bill would have him slotted to line up one place on the field and Hollywood would line up another place. Henderson drove him crazy. Guessing, moving around the field like a free spirit by whim, those were Hollywood's trademarks.

I became fairly friendly with Hollywood, who was a

likable guy. And he was fond of telling me and most anyone else who would listen all about his problems.

"Stroker," he'd say, as I remember it, "I made $100,000 or more doing that Seven-Up commercial, but I never saw a penny of it. I spent all the dough on cocaine. I went through girls, wives, cash, whatever. I wasn't doing drugs. Drugs were doing me."

"That's too bad," I told him.

"Yeah," he said. "But I should have realized how bad it was when I got my first hint that I needed help."

"When was that?"

"When my girl friend gave me a telescope and I got up at four in the morning and focused the damn thing on the moon and saw the American flag."

One night Hollywood joined me and a bunch of the guys at a restaurant for dinner. Here's the scenario I remember. "Stroker," he gave me that big smile of his. "Could you loan me twenty-five bucks? I'm a little bit short. I'll pay you back when we get paid."

I loaned him the money, and he left the table. There were about a dozen of us there shooting the breeze and getting into the mood for dinner. Then Henderson came back and ordered three shots of tequila. He took one and drank it. He took another and poured it on his salad. Then he swirled the last one around and around for a couple of minutes, put it in his beer and downed it.

We all ordered dinner, and everyone got his fill. The checks came around. "Don," he said. "I have a problem."

"What's the problem?"

"I don't have any money."

"Hollywood, I just lent you money."

"Yeah, but I had to buy the babes over at the bar a couple of drinks. Buy my dinner. I'll get you Tuesday, payday."

I bought him dinner. Like I said, he was such a likable guy.

Then there was the time before a preseason game when I lent him my car, which had a full tank of gas. He brought the car back without a scratch on it. I was pleased. Usually, I left for games at the last minute so I could beat the traffic. Well, I got into the car and started it up. The needle was on empty. I was pissed and just lucky enough to drive to the corner gas station.

When I arrived at the stadium, I ran into Hollywood. "Listen, Thomas..." he didn't like to be called that. He loved "Hollywood." "What's the deal about leaving my car on empty?"

"I'm sorry." He gave me that big grin. "I didn't even notice."

It was hard to notice that Hollywood was on the Dolphins, his time there was so brief before he got cut. I don't know how serious he was about making the team anyway. Later on he made some news being accused of raping a paraplegic in California. It takes a real "man" to do that. He was convicted and sent to jail for a time. When he was released, he started making speeches about the evils of drugs and alcohol for a fee. Then he wrote his book, which you could say did have an appropriate title: *Out of Control.*

Bob Hayes, the old Dallas Cowboy, was another player who also screwed up his life and also like Hollywood wrote a book. On the back cover of the Bob Hayes book is this quote from Hollywood Henderson: "I enjoyed

Run, Bullet, Run, and as a former pro athlete and recovering alcoholic, I related to Bob's story from start to finish. It's about hope after drugs, alcohol and mistakes. Like *Out of Control* Bob's story should be read by every black athlete in America."

You scratch my back and I'll scratch your... The whole way guys like Hollywood Henderson and the others act and are treated makes me sick.

There was also Stanley Wilson of the Bengals, supposedly doing drugs the night before the Super Bowl in Miami.

Now Hollywood, Hayes, and others are out there networking like guys who have suddenly found the light. It seems to me they are shamelessly giving true confessions, just like Kitty Dukakis, about the evils and horrors of their ways—and making big money doing it.

What is the message being sent by all of this? How can I go to an elementary or junior high school and say to the kids, "Just say no to drugs," when there are guys who didn't say no, like Dexter Manley, who was making $480,000 a year, supposedly banned for life from the game, out for one year and then back in. If you get sent to jail for life imprisonment, you don't get out in a year. But in the NFL if you're caught and have good talent, they'll take care of you.

Only in America and in the National Football League can things like this happen.

BEST

OF THE

BEST

IN the ever changing world of professional football, everybody has a list of all-stars, top performers, personal favorites. Fans favor some guys; the people who cover the NFL have their own criteria. Players talk a lot about whom they respect the most.

Many of the picks for these "dream teams," top pro selections, what have you, are a product of media hype, exposure on television, how a guy's team does. Howard Cosell made the reputations of a lot of players by taking a liking to them and talking about them over and over again. Some guys wound up with big reputations even though they didn't deserve it. And others were overlooked for one reason or another.

I've got my own thoughts about the "Best of the Best." My picks are based on seventeen years of being there on the scene in the National Football League, seeing players in their prime, going against them head to head, watching weeks of film, standing on the sidelines seeing how guys performed in the heat of a game.

There's no media bias in my picks, but I do admit there may be a bit of Miami Dolphin feeling that found its way into my selections.

So here they are—Don Strock's "Best of the Best."

QUARTERBACKS

1. Joe Namath
2. Dan Marino

Joe Willie Namath is one of my all-time favorite players. The way he carried himself on the field, the way he performed in New York with not very good football teams, the transition he made to the Rams and what he did with the quarterbacks there—the whole package was something special. Joe did so much, all the while being physically crippled. The white shoes, the air he had about him, there was no mistaking that was Joe Willie in the game dropping back to throw, delivering the pass—that was style.

From the time Joe Willie guaranteed that he would win the 1969 Super Bowl for the Jets, a 17-point underdog against the Baltimore Colts and Don Shula, and he did, every game Joe played until he retired Shula never trusted him. We played the Jets a game in the Orange Bowl and were up by 17 points with a couple of minutes to go. I said to Don Shula: "It looks pretty good."

And Shula said: "I don't trust that guy."

And sure enough Namath threw something like an 88-yard touchdown pass to Rich Caster.

And Shula said: "I told you."

So against Namath, Shula never called the horses off, never played loose zone. He played good solid defense the whole game against that guy.

185

Now they're all talking about the quickest release since Namath. This and that, since Namath. I don't think Joe ever fully got his due. Being in New York and getting all the publicity about Bachelors Three, and hanging out all night—the media there just ate that up. Sure Joe made statements like "I really love football. As far as I'm concerned it's the second best thing in the world." And "I like my girls blonde and my Johnny Walker Red." *But there is no guy who hangs out all night and can perform the way he did!*

Today when they talk about the skills of quarterbacks, they say, "He's got quick feet like Namath," or "His release is almost as fast as Joe Willie's." But there was just one Joe Willie Namath. He had all the tools and the heart and brain to go with them.

Joe Willie has said that Dan Marino is the best quarterback he's ever seen play in the NFL. Dan is like Joe was. There are lots of things they have in common—both out of Pennsylvania, both with the braces, both leaders with that will to win. The drop back in the pocket is a little different, but there's no mistaking when you saw Joe drop back and when you see Dan drop back who they are.

Dan Marino now is right in the middle of his prime, putting it all together. He has an excellent football mind and retains things very well. Dan is one of the greatest competitors that I've played with, and whether he's down by 21 or up by 21, he keeps the pressure on himself and the opposition. He has a need to win. That's in football, golf, cards, whatever.

Every year with Dan Marino there are the trade rumors. After the football season is over, Dan and I usually spend time together at the Pebble Beach Golf Tourney. Then he goes to see Shula. And there have been a few times that he has asked to be traded. Since I haven't been there the past few years, I am the scapegoat. "How come," Shula always tells him, "you always ask to be traded after coming back from playing in the golf tournament with your buddy?" It's not me—it's Dan. He wants the opportunity to get back to the Super Bowl and to win.

John Elway, Warren Moon, Randall Cunningham, and some others can throw the ball farther than Dan, but it's not so much distance anymore. If a quarterback has to sit in the pocket and throw the ball over forty yards, he's bound to get hit. In Miami it's more of a timing thing anyway, throwing to holes. Dan doesn't throw perfect spirals, but he has power and great touch on the ball. Warming up on the sidelines he is always so pumped up throwing bullets that he'll be hurting guys' hands. He feels like he can throw against anybody at any time.

At 6 feet 4 inches and 225 pounds, Dan is very strong. In the pocket he has great mobility and doesn't get sacked very much and has the quickest release of the ball since Joe Namath. He can feel pressure. On the field he shows emotion, and that is something he's working on. He's been known to holler at teammates and stuff. Dan tries to be a perfectionist.

But Dan is well liked by his teammates and even by the opposition, who respect him for what he's done. You won't see players taking a lot of cheap shots on him.

Very few quarterbacks have ever made the people

around them better. That's what he does with the Dolphins. My view of Dan Marino may be biased, but could Joe Montana play with the Dolphins and go 12–4? I say no way, and as great as Joe Montana is, I still put him in my list of the "3s" behind Dan Marino and Joe Namath.

Number 3s.

Joe Montana won four Super Bowls in the 1980s, and his record speaks for itself. What he's done in big games is better than John Wayne's accomplishments in movie shootouts. But Don Shula always said that Bob Griese was better driving a Cadillac than a Chevrolet. The same is true of Joe Montana. He was a third-round pick out of Notre Dame, a kind of late bloomer. For a few years, he was not doing that much, but once the people around him got better, he got better at quarterback.

The first time Dwight Clark saw Montana he asked: "Who is this, the punter?" Like Bob Griese, Montana is not a very big guy, not a physical type of player. But he's very smart and takes advantage of what the opposition gives him and is a master at running the two-minute drill. Montana is the closest today to Bob Griese as a thinking man's quarterback who gets the most out of his ability. Joe has won a lot of games that he should've lost. And although I rank him behind Joe Namath and Dan Marino, I put him ahead of Terry Bradshaw and Bob Griese in my "Best of the Best."

Fran Tarkenton was a master. He didn't throw the ball deep down the field often, but he was a great scrambler. "When everything else breaks down," he used to say, "I don't hesitate to roam out of the pocket and do the bugaloo." That was good for his day. Today, if you roam out of the pocket, there are guys who are bigger, stronger, and sometimes faster than you, and you get nailed. But Fran was more than just a scrambler. He liked the short and the intermediate-distance passes, and he made them work for him. He ended up with the most touchdowns, most yardage. The shame of it all was that he never won the Super Bowl, even though he got there four times.

Terry Bradshaw was kind of the opposite side of the quarterback coin. He liked to throw the ball deep and had tremendous receivers in Lynn Swann and John Stallworth who could get out there and catch some balls. Terry made a lot of big plays in games, but he also made a lot of mistakes in games. But with the defense they had, the Steelers could cover up for that. Hell, how can you be critical of Terry Bradshaw? He ended up winning four Super Bowls.

Between Tarkenton and Bradshaw—that's seven Super Bowls. One guy won four; one guy lost three. But they're both in the Hall of Fame. And rightfully so. I played against both of them—Fran at the end of his career and Terry before injuries ended his time in the NFL.

Bob Griese is a dear friend of mine and ran a team like a clock, but like Joe Montana, Bob couldn't win games on his own. If you put Griese on the Jets in those years they were in the league together and Joe Willie with Miami, everything would have been reversed.

I pair Johnny Unitas with Griese as quarterbacks. Neither had the great individual talent, but both of them didn't make a lot of mistakes. They also knew how to win. It was Johnny U. who said: "A quarterback hasn't arrived until he can tell the coach to go to hell." And Johnny told a lot of them to do that.

Another who could win was Roger Staubach. Roger Staubach was a master at running the two-minute drill, like Johnny Unitas, George Blanda, and Joe Montana. And Roger, like those guys, used every person on the field to the top of his ability.

Kenny Stabler used to brag: "I studied many a game plan by the light of the jukebox." He must have done a lot of studying, because he won many football games for the Raiders and was unsung for all he did, and he did a lot. Stabler and I had the same philosophy. You don't need twenty-two plays on third down to run third down. He used to go into a game with three or four. Seeing him on TV today he looks much older than he really is. But come to think of it, maybe he always looked that old.

Sonny Jurgensen is in the Hall of Fame and he should be. He was a competitor. I remember playing against him in Washington, and he beat us in the last six seconds by throwing a short touchdown pass. That broke our back, but he was another extremely talented quarterback and you always had to respect the guy's will to win.

I give a tip of my cap to Boomer Esiason and Jim Kelly as great competitors. And I can't leave out Bert Jones on my list of backup quarterbacks in the Best of the Best. Bert was in my draft in 1973. It was just too bad that he had a world of ability cut down by injury.

Naturally, John Elway is also on the list. A great

athlete and a great talent, he's 0–3 in Super Bowls. But he's been there and there are a lot on this list who never have been. He has time.

Bernie Kosar is today's thinking man's quarterback—not the greatest athlete in the world, a guy who looks very unorthodox out there on the field, but he gets it done.

Dan Fouts, Warren Moon, Randall Cunningham—those guys belong on the list here, too. Fouts labored with a not so excellent team, but he got the Chargers into the play-offs several times and is second on the all-time passing list. I still remember how magnificent he was in the shootout I had against him in the "Greatest Game of the 1980s." Cunningham, absolutely without question, is the greatest athlete at the quarterback position to have ever played the game. At one point in the 1990 season he had been responsible for 82 percent of the Eagles' total offense.

Another guy in my "3" category is Billy Kilmer, who probably had less athletic ability than all of the quarterbacks I've discussed. He had a bad leg, his body didn't look like he should have been playing football, and he probably didn't throw more than a half-dozen spirals in his NFL career—and that was just when he got lucky. But he was a winner and probably the greatest leader of all these guys I've mentioned. And that includes Joe Willie Namath.

You'll notice there are only two black quarterbacks on my list, Moon and Cunningham. There haven't been that many through the history of the NFL. There are more today, with guys like Andre Ware, Rodney Peete, Don McPherson.

Maybe there should be more black quarterbacks, more black coaches, etc. The fact is that in college a lot of the black quarterbacks are sprint-out types, not pocket passers, and that's why quite a few of them who star in college don't make it in the NFL.

If a man is qualified and shows he can play, he should be hired. The final decision on who is hired to play in the NFL is not made by the press or the players; it's twenty-eight coaches who make that decision; it's twenty-eight owners who make the decision on the coaches.

Then the game goes on—black and white together, bruised together, bleeding together. And in the end you win together or you lose together.

FULLBACKS

1. Larry Csonka. After reading all I had to say about him in other parts of this book, you know why I have him up at number one.

2. John Riggins is remembered more by some people for the Mohawk hairdo and the way he acted, sort of jumping to the beat of a different drummer. People still remember when he passed out under the table and told Sandra Day O'Connor, the Supreme Court Justice: "Hey, baby, relax a little bit." John wasn't the relaxed type, but he could catch the ball, could block, and could run very well. He's one of the top ten leading rushers of all time.

3. Franco Harris was never big on taking the extra hit the way Csonka and Riggins were. Franco would step out of bounds. But he played up there in Pittsburgh in the cold weather, and he could grind it out. A very low-key, soft-spoken guy, Franco was the heart and soul of the Steelers.

HALFBACKS

1. Hands down it's Walter Payton. The all-time NFL leading rusher and a guy who sacrificed himself so many ways for his team, Walter was a great blocker who also caught the ball very well. He played hard all the time.

My other choices here are

2A. Tony Dorsett
2B. Eric Dickerson
3A. Earl Campbell
3B. Marcus Allen

Dickerson and Dorsett didn't block. Earl didn't like to do it too often, and neither does Marcus. But running the ball? All of them are in another league.

Of the whole group of running backs, the two toughest were Payton and Csonka. They could lift a team.

My asterisk choice as a "Best of the Best" running back is Bo Jackson. At one point in the 1990 season he had gained 600 yards in five weeks of play. That was after he had played a full season of baseball with the Kansas City Royals, after coming to the Raider training camp a little late. Jackson has talent he hasn't even discovered yet. The guy is just oozing with it. Only time will tell how great he can become. And he's already been recognized by being picked as an alternate in the

1991 Pro Bowl, after having been on the American League All-Star baseball team. That gives Bo the distinction of being the only guy in the modern era to make an all-star team in two pro sports.

WIDE RECEIVER

1. Paul Warfield
2. Steve Largent

My 3s include Nat Moore, John Stallworth, Mark Duper, Mark Clayton, James Lofton, Jerry Rice, Lynn Swann, Stanley Morgan, and Fred Biltnikoff.

Paul Warfield was one of the few receivers who could dictate the coverage, and that gave whoever was quarterbacking an idea of what would happen. Double-teamed, he caught a lot of balls. Paul was probably the best blocker at wide receiver ever. When he came into the NFL out of Ohio State, he came from a program where they did not throw the ball that much. But Paul was such a natural talent he taught himself how to be a great receiver.

Steve Largent was picked up by Seattle after the Cowboys let him go. No one really imagined what he would turn into. Playing hurt, always finding a way to get open, a guy with great moves—you'd look at the film of what he was able to do, and you had to respect Steve Largent.

Nat Moore was a running back at the University of Florida. When he came to the Dolphins, his locker was right next to that of Paul Warfield. Day in and day out Moore questioned Paul and learned from him. Years later Duper and Clayton did the same thing with Nat, learning all they could about patterns and reads. So there was a line from Warfield to Moore to Clayton and Duper.

John Stallworth and Lynn Swann made many big plays for the Steelers through the years.

James Lofton and Stanley Morgan were guys who could really fly. Lofton is still with the Buffalo Bills and Morgan is now with the Colts.

Jerry Rice is a tremendous athlete with great speed and a knack for making the big plays in the big games.

Fred Biletnikoff wasn't the fastest, most physical, or best athlete but he ran precise routes and made big catches.

TIGHT ENDS

1. Kellen Winslow
1A. Russ Francis
1B. Ozzie Newsome
1C. Dave Casper

Kellen Winslow was a big, strong guy and he could run. In the San Diego scheme that he played in, he was a good enough blocker. All around he was the best tight end I ever saw. It's a shame the way his career was ended by an injury.

Russ Francis was a sky diver who flew his own plane, a surfer, a free spirit, a great football talent. For all I know he's probably floating around in the sky on a hang glider right now.

Ozzie Newsome, whom I played with when I was at Cleveland, was the real life Wizard of Oz. Once he caught a pass from Ronald Reagan, who came to practice one day. "That's the first time," Ozzie joked, "I caught a pass thrown by somebody older than Don Strock." That statement is not the reason I put Ozzie 1B, but, Oz, it's better than being number 3.

Dave Casper was voted as the starting tight end on the All-Time Super Bowl Team. Not a great blocker, Dave read patterns real well and knew how to get open. His quarterbacks could always find him.

OFFENSIVE TACKLES

As a quarterback I didn't spend a whole lot of time on the sidelines watching other teams' offensive tackles. But there were a few of those guys who stood out for me through the long seasons.

1. Art Shell
2. Anthony Munoz
3A. Jackie Slater
3B. Mike Kenn

Art Shell was a ferocious and huge man who played left tackle next to left guard Gene Upshaw. That was quite a combination on the Raiders, being a left-handed team with Kenny Stabler at quarterback. The Raiders would run to that side a lot, the way many teams do, making their moves by the quarterback's hand position. But having the game plan to sweep down behind Art Shell made him and the Raiders something special. Munoz of Cincinnati is like a Pete Rose type, a guy whose name you just chalked in and let him play. Kenn is a very big man who blocked out the sun for more than a decade. Jackie Slater of the Rams has been to numerous pro bowls and is currently starting his sixteenth season.

OFFENSIVE GUARDS

1. John Hannah
1A. Larry Little
1B. Gene Upshaw
1C. Bob Kuechenberg

John Hannah was hard to get around. For a big guy he was a great power blocker on the run. Anytime his team needed a yard, everybody in the league knew they would be running behind John. He made very few mistakes. Larry Little was very underrated at pulling guard. He was a leader, a team captain and very much faster than a lot of people thought. Gene Upshaw, who went on to become head of the NFL Players Association, was steady, intelligent, quick, and durable. He was always a good union man, but that's not why I've picked him. The Pro Football Hall of Fame picked him way ahead of me. Kuch was a tough guy, very strong. His father made a living at fairs being shot out of a cannon. And Kuechenberg seemed to be coming out of a cannon when he went after opposing players.

CENTER

1. Dwight Stephenson and Jim Langer (tie)
1A. Jim Otto and Mike Webster (tie)

The center position is something I knew real well. As I said before I felt more ass there than I felt anywhere else. And I still remember all the gas that was passed at me in practice on purpose by Dwight and Jim. But even though centers kid around a lot, they're got a tough job out there. They give all the calls for the offensive line, know all the blocking patterns, have to know the cadence, have to snap the ball and make all the adjustments. It's not as easy position by any means. And playing for those teams that use the shotgun makes it even tougher. Silent counts away from home in a domed stadium are something else still that make the center job a tough one.

Jim Langer was there when I joined the Dolphins in 1973 and was on the scene until 1978–79, when he and his wife decided that they didn't want to raise their children in south Florida and Shula traded him to Minnesota for a low-round draft pick. Quick afoot, a guy with a strong frame, Jim played excellent football every down. He was also one of those guys who could endure pain. He had a screw in his knee and it came loose. They improvised by banging a hammer against a board placed on Jim's knee.

Jim asked the doctor, "Have you ever done this before?"

The answer: "No, but this looks like it might work." It did.

Dwight Stephenson was a strong, tough guy who handled the nose guard all by himself. Against three-man lines we always had a free back or lineman to help against the linebacker when blitzing came. Most teams in that situation have to slide the line one way or the other. Dwight was just an outstanding center and a good guy; it was a shame the way he ended his career. We were playing the Jets and Marty Lyons hit him from the side. Dwight had his leg planted. The hit caused nerve damage and totally destroyed Dwight's knee. It was ironic that Marty Lyons was the one who did it. Both he and Dwight were teammates at the University of Alabama and were very good friends.

It was always comforting to have Dwight Stephenson and Jim Langer bending down in front of me, even if they did sometimes leave wind. I also would not have minded Jim Otto or Mike Webster. Jim played for the Raiders and never missed a game in years and years. He wound up with two plastic knees, a plastic hip, the works. Mike Webster was in the middle of the Pittsburgh line that used the quick trap as a weapon. He was another center who did an excellent job for what seemed like forever. In 1990, he was still plying his trade for the KC Chiefs. Mike was hired as a line coach by Marty Schottenheimer and still had something left, so he moved back into his old starting center role.

DEFENSIVE ENDS

Defensive end is the position that has undergone the most changes since I came into the game. It's gotten the greatest athletes and is the toughest defensive position to play. Guys who play there have to stop the run, rush the passer, contend with receivers in motion who might crack-back on them, deal with backs in motion who come back and chop on them. It was a stationary position to play, and guys basically lined up game after game in the same place. If they were positioned at right defensive end, that's where they played. Today defensive ends move—left side, right side, over center. Many times they are standing up and they get that momentum and run and shoot a gap. It's not a pretty sight for an opposing quarterback or any of the players on offense.

My picks at that position combine speed, power, quickness, strength, size—and the attitude to get out there and make it all happen.

1. Reggie White
1A. Bruce Smith
2. Howie Long
2A. Carl Eller

Reggie White is in a class by himself. He breaks down the pocket as good as anyone ever did, and lines up all over the place—center, whatever, something like Bruce Smith. Reggie's long arms make it difficult to throw around him. Bruce Smith went to Virginia Tech, and there's just a thin line that separates him from Reggie. They both wreak havoc. Carl Eller was a big man, quick and intimidating. They called him "the Moose." He was another guy who knew how to break down the pocket and was one of the key ingredients of the Minnesota "Purple People Eaters" defense. My backups at defensive end include Claude Humphrey, Atlanta; L. C. Greenwood, Pittsburgh, an outside rusher like Smith; and Jack Youngblood, LA Rams, a guy who was great at his position and who never got enough credit for the job he did.

DEFENSIVE TACKLES

1. Alan Page
1A. Mean Joe Greene.

These picks may surprise some people. My starters are Alan Page, Minnesota, a great pass rusher and the first defensive lineman to be an MVP in the NFL, and "Mean Joe" Greene, who with the old Steelers just lined up sideways in the gap and came on, came on. Oh, how those two guys could contain, handle reverses, intimidate an offense. The rest of the depth chart includes Randy White of Dallas; Joe Klecko out of Temple University, who cracked my ribs; Merlin Olsen, whom I saw at the end of his career and on some very impressive film clips. Merlin has great technique today as a TV commentator and had it back when he was playing. Curly Culp rounds out the group. He was short, squat, wide, and very strong. Jim Langer hated to play against Curly and claimed he had the best forearm shiver of any nose tackle he ever played against. Curly was a tough son of a bitch, and with him out on the field it was war all the time. For a four-man line my tackles are Greene and Page, but with a three-man line I'd go to Culp and Klecko at nose tackles.

OUTSIDE LINEBACKERS

Here I have to modify things a little bit. In a four-three defense I pick Jack Ham and Andy Russell. In a three-four set I would have to go with Lawrence Taylor and Ted Hendricks.

Jack Ham controlled the tight end as well as anybody who ever played the game, and he played his position to the tilt against most of the teams of his time, which were right-handed in formation. Andy Russell covered the back out of the backfield as well as anybody ever did. It seemed we could never complete a pass against him. If we went to a left-side formation, Ham covered as well as Russell. Ham is in the Hall of Fame. I just can't understand why Russell isn't there, too.

L.T. and the man they called "the Stork," Ted Hendricks seem perfect to me as a tandem, for the three-four. Lawrence plays at 110 percent all the time. Double-teamed, tripled-teamed, somehow he gets there. Hendricks is my neighbor in Miami Springs. He played at 6 feet 7, 6 feet 8, 225 pounds, and with that incredible arm span you could never throw around him. Ted was a master at reading your offensive set and more times than not would know where the play was going. He always tipped a lot of balls and holds the all-time record for blocked kicks of field goals and extra points. Part of that was due to his size and his arm span; part of it came from great football instincts.

For either set at outside linebacker, my depth chart includes Andre Tippet, Matt Blair, and Cornelius Bennett.

INSIDE LINEBACKERS

1. Dick Butkus
1. Jack Lambert

My picks here are both Hall of Famers—Dick Butkus and Jack Lambert. Butkus, as I said, I saw only at the end of his career, but I saw him on film and heard the veterans talk about him a lot. He was a piece of work who played search and destroy. The man was speed and power and a frightening sight out there. Jack Lambert is deservedly in the Hall of Fame. A second-round pick out of Kent State, Jack was a fierce competitor. He was still playing when they put in the rule to protect the quarterbacks. "Why not put a skirt on them," he asked, "if you want to give them protection?"

In the four-three, the backup player for me is Tommy Nobis, "the General," who starred for Atlanta. In the three-four, it's Nick Buoniconti out of Notre Dame, my teammate on Miami. He was a very small player at 5 feet 10 and less than 210 pounds. Nick was a really sharp guy who could diagram the offensive set and call all the changes in the defense with the best of them. Another backup is Steve Wilson of New England. He played hurt all the time, was a quarterback on defense. In many ways he was a player very similar to Buoniconti. Honorable mention: Mike Singletary—a great player for the Chicago Bears.

CORNERBACKS

1. Mike Haynes
1. Mel Blount
1A. Lester Hayes
1B. Raymond Claiborne
1C. Willie Brown

I'd take any of these guys any time. Mel Blount and Smooth Mike Haynes always received a lot of publicity. Mike was a guy we on the Dolphins didn't like to throw against very much. Willie Brown belongs on the depth chart. He was a great cover guy with the Raiders and was an assistant coach with the late George Allen at Long Beach State University.

STRONG SAFETIES

1. Ken Houston
1A. Donnie Shell
1B. Charlie Waters

Ken Houston is at the top of the hill here because he was a big guy, a guy who had the ability to come up and stop the run and also play the pass. He has lots of all-time records for strong safety, many of those set with the Houston Oilers. Then George Allen made a great trade and acquired Houston to solidify the strong safety position for the Redskins. Allen also picked up Jake Scott for weak safety. He teamed Houston and Scott up, two tremendous safeties picked up for virtually nothing.

Donnie Shell was on four Super Bowl winners with Pittsburgh. This was a guy who read pass patterns very well and was a great hitter. Charlie Waters was not a great hitter, but he got the job done time after time. He was especially excellent performing the safety blitz.

Honorable mention goes to my Dolphin teammate Dick Anderson and to Doug Plank of the Chicago Bears, a player they named a whole defensive set after—the "46" defense. Doug wore number 46 and was one of the most uncontrollable hitters of all.

WEAK SAFETIES

1. Jake Scott
2. Mike Wagner

For me, there's no real competition. It's Jake Scott all the way. Jake played for Miami in the Super Bowl against Washington with two broken ribs and was the MVP—and won a car and traded it in for a truck. A big-play guy, a safety blitzer, Jake was small but played the game all out. If he was there as the last one to the goal line, Jake seldom missed the guy. Mike Wagner of Pittsburgh was one of the most intelligent guys at his position; he made few mistakes. He made the calls in the secondary and was superb at reading patterns. If someone was lucky enough to catch a ball, Mike was the last guy to the goal line—and he seemed to always make the stop. My backups include Nolan Cromwell of the Rams, Gary Fencik of the Bears, and Deron Cherry of Kansas City, the interception leader for several years, a man with a good nose for the football.

PUNTER

1. Ray Guy—by himself

Ray was one of the most exceptional athletes I've ever seen. The first time I saw him was when I was in college. We came out the same year. Ray played quarterback for Southern Miss against my Virginia Tech team. He also played weak safety and intercepted one of my passes. In his prime in the NFL he was a holder for kicks and also a guy who kicked off, but he earned his money and his reputation as a punter—and he could kick the hell out of the football and lay it down where he wanted it.

PLACEKICKERS

1. George Blanda
1A. Garo Yepremian
1B. Jim Bakken
1C. Jan Stenerud
1D. Morton Anderson
1E. Tom Dempsey

Without question my number one is George Blanda. There was never a performer like George under the gun. In his twenty-sixth year he was still kicking winning field goals. Very accurate, a straight-on conventional kicker, Blanda knew what he had to do. I've never seen another quarterback throw the ball down the field, get to the 20-yard line, and then kick the field goal to win. George Blanda did it many times. There was one season where he won three games in a row playing quarterback and kicking the ball. With 2,002 points to his credit, George is the leading lifetime scorer in professional football.

Morton Anderson is up there with George in percentage, but Blanda is in another sphere. Tom Dempsey belongs on the list. He did it by overcoming the handicap of playing with half a foot and went on to set the record with the longest field goal ever kicked. Honorable mention here goes to Nick Lowrey of Kansas City.

HEAD COACH

I could pick Chuck Knox. I could pick Tom Landry. I could pick a lot of guys. But I pick Don Shula.

One constant in Shula's life is that he's always had the knack and the ability to bring out the best in his players whether they were superstars or average talents. They all play under him to their full potential.

The nucleus of his coaching staff has been there for years. They all seem to think alike, with the same football philosophy. There are no real major changes in his game plans. He just tinkers a little. It's all blueprinted. His practice schedule is the same as it's been. You know what you're going to do every minute of every day. I guess all of that's a plus, because there isn't a football system that historically has been more successful, except maybe the Cowboys'. And Dallas and Miami are always compared.

We're also talking about a football guy who knows the score and through the years has piled up the stats to show that he can win with all kinds of teams.

Don Shula is an excellent coach, and for him to be there on the Dolphins that long with all those different personalities year in and year out takes a tremendous human being, especially in this day and age. He's now chasing the ghost of George Halas, and it's just a matter of time before Shula sets the record as the winningest coach in NFL history. My hat is off to him for being able to do it.

It's like Bubba Paris, the old 49ers' offensive tackle, said: "If a nuclear bomb is ever dropped on this country, the only things I'm certain will survive are Astro Turf and Don Shula."

CAREER STATISTICS

Year	Att.	Cmp.	Yds.	Pct.	TDs	Int.
1973 (Miami) did not play						
1974 ''	0	0	0	0	0	0
1975 ''	45	26	230	57.8	2	2
1976 ''	47	21	359	44.7	3	2
1977 ''	4	2	12	50.0	0	1
1978 ''	135	72	825	53.3	12	6
1979 ''	100	56	830	56.0	6	6
1980 ''	62	30	313	48.4	1	5
1981 ''	130	79	901	60.1	6	8
1982 ''	55	30	306	54.5	2	5
1983 ''	52	34	403	65.4	4	1
1984 ''	6	4	27	66.7	0	0
1985 ''	9	7	141	77.8	1	0
1986 ''	20	14	152	70.0	2	0
1987 ''	23	13	114	56.5	0	1
Totals (Miami)	688	388	4613	56.4	39	37
1988 (Cle)	91	55	736	60.4	6	5

CAREER HIGHLIGHTS

1973 Fifth-round draft choice (No. 111 overall) by the Dolphins out of Virginia Tech.

1975 Starts first game Dec. 7 against Buffalo when Bob Griese and Earl Morrall are injured. Completes 12 of 15 passes, including 11 in a row, in 31–21 victory.

1978 Starts first seven games after Griese tears knee ligaments in preseason. Connects on 65 of 125 attempts as Dolphins go 5–2.

1980 Keys rally from nine-point deficit to defeat Cincinnati, 17–16.

1982 Best-remembered game. Enters play-off against San Diego in second quarter with Dolphins trailing, 24–0. Completes 29 of 43 passes for 403 yards and four touchdowns, but Dolphins lose, 41–38, in OT.

1985 Teams with Mark Duper for longest completion of his career, 67 yards, against Houston.

1987 Plays in all 12 nonstrike games (some just as a holder) with no starts. Is called upon to punt for the first time in NFL career when Reggie Roby goes down with injury against New England. Has seven punts for 33.6-yard average in rainstorm, and three are downed inside Patriots' 20.

INDEX

ABOUT THE AUTHOR

Harvey Frommer has written more than thirty sports books and over six hundred articles. His most recent books include autobiographies of Red Holzman, Nolan Ryan, and Tony Dorsett. He also is the author of *Growing Up at Bat: 50 Years of Little League Baseball*. Together with his wife, Myrna, he recently wrote *It Happened in the Catskills*, an oral history of the resort phenomenon.

He is the guest curator and executive producer of "Stars of David: Jews in Sports," an exhibit that opened in the spring of 1991 at the B'nai B'rith Museum in Washington, D.C.